Tarot

How to Read Tarot Cards and Master Astrology, the Zodiac Signs, and Tap into Your Psychic Abilities

Free limited time bonus

Stop for a moment. I have a free bonus set up for you. The problem is that we forget 90% of everything that we read after 7 days. Crazy fact, right? Here's the solution: we've created a printable, 1-page pdf summary for this book that you're reading now. All you have to do to get your free pdf summary is to go to the following website: **https://livetolearn.lpages.co/silviahill/** Once you do, it will be intuitive. Enjoy, and thank you!

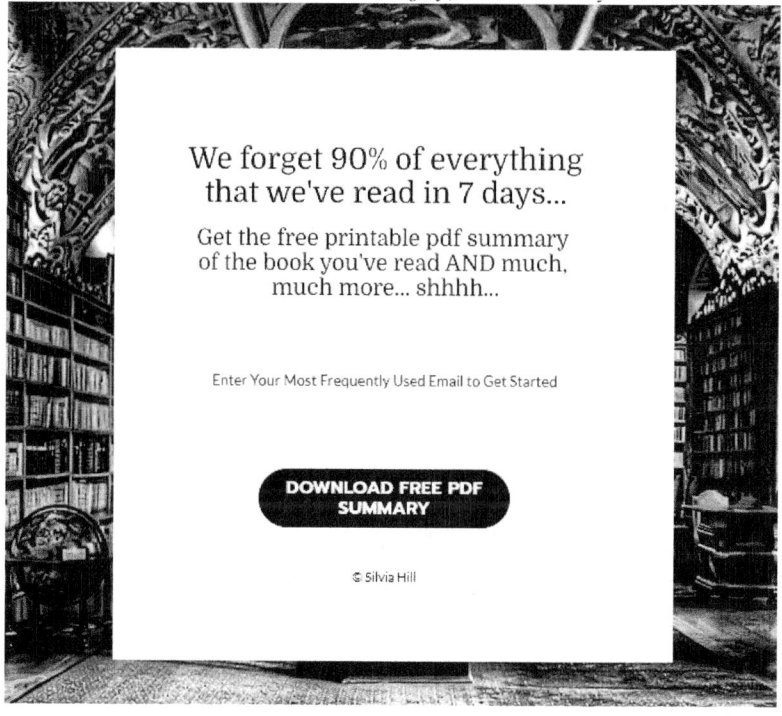

We forget 90% of everything that we've read in 7 days...

Get the free printable pdf summary of the book you've read AND much, much more... shhhh...

Enter Your Most Frequently Used Email to Get Started

DOWNLOAD FREE PDF SUMMARY

© Silvia Hill

Contents

Introduction

Many people assume that the world has neither rhyme nor reason, but that's not the case at all, as you'll discover in this book. There is a way to glean the meaning behind the patterns that play out in life. Life itself is like a movie, a narrative of narratives, where you have individual stories playing out within the context of a collective, grander story.

Movies follow a plan. That's the script. When you read one, you'll notice that each character and prop has a distinct role to play. Each action they take and the choices they make will inevitably culminate in the grand conclusion of the movie. The characters, their actions, motivations, props, and the other elements of their world form a pattern, if you will. When you look at these pieces individually, they may not immediately make sense at the beginning but, by the end, they click, and you can see the pattern that connects them all. The individual pictures that make up the movie come together and, by the end, it's obvious to you why they did. You can't imagine them playing out any other way.

What's all this talk about movies and patterns? Life is like a movie, except not everyone is lucky enough to know how it ends for them. Having said that, you can find the patterns that light up your path on the journey of your life. They may not show you the destination, but fortunately, what matters more is the journey, cliché as that sounds. There are numerous ways to determine your path, gain insight into what you can do to improve it, and find fulfillment along the way. One of the many ways you can access the script of your life is to work with tarot.

Unfortunately, the tarot has been misunderstood and maligned for far too long, especially as humans have become more modern and more and more things can be explained by science. However, science doesn't have all the answers yet, and where science fails, other tools like the tarot can offer us the answers we seek to questions science doesn't answer.

You're going to find that this book is very practical. You'll learn all you need to know about the tarot, how to read these cards, and how they're connected with astrology and the zodiac signs. This book also teaches you how to connect with your psychic abilities and develop them so you can use them in everyday life. Whether you already have some experience with tarot or are completely new to it, you will find all you need to know within these pages. By the end of the book, you'll realize that there's much more to these cards than you've been told and that, used correctly, they can bring you a life-changing level of insight that will leave you ever thankful you picked up this book out of all the others available on the subject.

If you're ready to get to know yourself on a level you've never even contemplated before, get ready for the ride of your life. By working with the tarot pictures and meanings, you'll also better understand the people around you and the world at large. So, fasten your seatbelt, and let's get started.

PART ONE: Tarot and Astrology Basics

Chapter 1: Introduction to Tarot

As Fraulein Maria once trilled, "*Let's start from the very beginning; a very good place to start.*" Let's begin our journey by talking about what tarot is.

Etymological Root

Tarot is pronounced *tah-roh*, and the Germanic *tarock* is from the Italian word *tarocchi*. It's unclear what the root of the Italian word is, but back in the 15th and 16th centuries, *taroch* meant "foolishness." In the 15th century, the deck of cards was called "*troonfi,.*" a name that popped up around 1503 in Brescia, as people began calling the cards "*tarocho.*" By the 16th century, there was a new game that went by a similar name, and it was called trionfa. At the same time, the older form of the cards was called *tarocchi.*

In present-day Italian, *tarocco* is the word for a blood orange cultivar. Along with the noun taroccare, this term describes forgeries or fakes. The meaning comes from the tarocchi game itself, as it was enjoyed in Italy, where the tarocco was a card you could play in lieu of a different card.

Cultural and Historical Background

This is a deck of playing cards from the middle of the 15th century that became popular across parts of Europe. People used them to play games like tarot from France, Konigrufen from Austria, and tarocchini from Italy. Many of the games played with tarot back then are still played even now.

There are different tarot decks, and by the 18th century, certain decks were being used in cartomancy to offer people divinatory readings. This led to other decks being created strictly to help with occult matters. They are used all over Europe regularly, rather than being for occult purposes. In other English-speaking regions where these games aren't common, the cards are mostly used for divination, and they have very special designs. It's believed that these cards may be connected to the I Ching, Indian Tantra, the Kabbalah, ancient Iran, and ancient Egypt.

These cards first came into Europe, with the very first records of them being in Berne in 1367, from where they spread like wildfire, likely because the games were banned at some point. There's not much known about how the cards looked at that time, except for what we know from John of Basle, also called Johannes Teuton or John of Rheinfelden, a Dominican writer and friar who wrote a description of the playing cards used in Europe. The text in question is from Freiburg im Breisgau, a city in Germany's Baden-Wurttemberg. Dated 1377, this text describes some of the cards, also talking about the courts of the King, Unter, Dames, Queens, and Ober, as well as the 4 suits made up of 13 cards.

Another style of tarot deck was used between 1440 and 1450, from Bologna, Florence, Ferrara, and Milan, and these card sets had extra trumps with allegorical drawings. These decks were called "triumph cards" or "cartes da trionfi," and the extra cards were the *trionfi* or trumps. The oldest tarot cards still around are the Visconti-Sforza decks. There are 15 of them, and they were created on behalf of those who ruled the Duchy of Milan.

There's a lost deck of cards resembling the tarot that Duke Filippo Maria Visconti had commissioned, which Martiano da Tortona described sometime between 1418 and 1425. According to his records, in 1418, a painter named Michelino da Besozzo came back to Milan. However, Maritano passed away in 1425. His description was of a deck with 60 cards, 16 of which were face cards of the Roman gods, with suits showing four types of birds, and 16 deemed as trumps.

Tarot decks are like regular playing cards, having four suits, and the presentation depends on the deck's region. In Northern Europe, you have the French suits, in Central Europe are the German suits, and in Southern Europe are the Latin suits. In each suit of the tarot, you'll find 14 cards. Ten of these cards are pip cards that go from one to ten, or ace to ten, with the ace being number one. The other four cards are face cards, also called court cards or royalty cards. They're called face cards because they have faces on them, specifically the faces of the Queen, King, Knight, and Page (or Knave or Jack).

You'll also find another trump suit of 21 cards in a tarot deck, as well as the Fool, making up the total of 22 cards. These cards make up the Major Arcana, and depending on which game you're playing, the Fool is either played as the top trump or to stop following the suit in play.

Tarot Decks

These cards weren't originally used for divination but for playing games. In one of Martiano da Tortona's manuscripts from before 1425, he outlines the rules of the game for a deck similar to the tarot. Two centuries after that, we get vague explanations of the terms and rules of the game until, of course, the oldest known rule description for a French version of the game in 1637. This game had many versions depending on the region in which it was played. In Bologna, tarocchini has managed to survive, and other forms of the game are played in Sicily and Piedmont.

By the 18th century, tarot was suddenly all the rage again, becoming very popular in Europe. The only places that didn't play with these cards were the Ottoman Balkans, the Iberian Peninsula, Britain, and Ireland. By the 1970s, there was another onslaught of tarot fever in France. Tarot games held across regions, called tarokk, tarok, or tarock, were also played all around central Europe and even within the old Austro-Hungarian Empire.

Italian Decks

These were the oldest sorts of tarot decks, with the earliest being from the 15th century, originating in northern Italy. There are three decks that, to date, have been used to play specific games. They are:

- **The Tarocco Bolognese**, which doesn't have the number cards from 2 to 5 in the plain suits, and only has 62 cards. Its trumps are also different from the norm, and not all of them are numbered. Four of the trumps have equal significance.
- **The Swiss 1JJ Tarot** is almost like the Tarocco Piemontese, but in place of the Pope, it has Jupiter, in place of the Popess is Juno, and in place of the Angel card is the

Judgment card. The significance of the trumps comes down to the numerical assignment, and instead of the Tower, you have the House of God. Also, these cards cannot be reversed.

• **The Tarocco Piemontese** has four suits of cups, coins, swords, and batons, and each suit is led by the Queen, King, Cavalier, and Jack. Then you have the pip cards as well, bringing the whole deck to 78 cards in total. The trump card is higher than 21 in many of the games, and the fool, while not a trump card, is numbered 0.

Italo-Portuguese Deck

The one deck that works with the Portuguese style of suits is the Tarocco Siciliano. It also works with Spanish pips, intersecting them in the same way as Italian pips. Among these trumps is the lowest one, known as the Miseria, which means "destitution." The two and three coins are omitted from this deck, as are the numbers one to four of the cups, swords, and clubs, bringing the total to 64 cards in the deck. The ace of coins isn't used in this deck, as it has the stamp tax. Also, these small cards are not reversible.

French Decks

There are various illustrations of these French suits, but they're different from the Italian suits, which are much older. They do away with the Renaissance allegories and designs. Other than some novelty decks, these card sets are mostly only used for card games. The very first set of French-suited decks had depictions of animals on the trump cards. This is why they were called *tiertarock*, from *tier*, which was the German word for "animal." These showed up sometime around 1740 and, by 1800, there were more forms of decks created with veduta (very detailed paintings) or genre art. These are the French-suited decks you can find these days:

• **Industrie un Gluck**: This means "diligence and fortune." From Central Europe, this deck uses Roman numerals on the trump cards. You'll find it has 54 cards, and the cards numbered 1 to 6 of the black suits are omitted, along with the ones numbered 5 to 10 of the red suits. You'll find three patterns – A, B, and C – and C is the standardized form of the cards, while the former two show up in special or limited editions.

- **Tarot Bourgeois:** This is also the Tarot Nouveau, and it has 78 cards. It's used for Danish tarot and French tarot games. It's also used for playing Cego in Germany. In its corners, indices are Arabic numerals.

- **Alder-Cego:** This is an animal tarot unique to the Upper Rhine Valley and the nearby mountainous regions, like the Vosges or the Black Forest. With 54 cards, it's organized in the same way as the Industrie und Gluck decks. At its center indices are Arabic numerals.

- **Schmid-Cego:** This pack was created by a German manufacturer, F. X. Schmid, who manufactured puzzles, board games, and playing cards. These cards have genre scenes (like depictions of everyday life in the markets, parties, streets, and so on) that are just like the ones you find in the Tarot Nouveau. However, it has Arabic numerals, which are centered.

German Decks

While there was a wider variety of German tarot decks of 78 cards, there are only two designs now, both of them based on Cego. These are the Cego by F. X. Schmid with genre scenes and Cego Adler designed by ASS Altenburger, a German manufacturer of playing cards.

You can also find other tarock cards for games like Bavarian tarock, Wurttemberg tarock, and Bauerntarock. These aren't actual tarot decks. However, the Wurttemberg or Bavarian patterns of these German decks only have 36 cards. These cards include the pip cards, which are numbered from 6 to 10, and the King, Ave, Ober or Over Knave, and Unter or Under Knave. These cards with the Ace to 10 ranking, where the Ace card is the most significant, followed not by 2 but by 10, then the King, Ober, Unter, and then 9 to 6. The trump suit here is the heart suit. People also use the Bavarian deck for playing Schafkopf, but they do so without the 6s across all suits.

Today's Decks

Today, we have three common decks of tarot:

- Marseille
- Rider Waite Smith
- Thoth

The Marseille Tarot

This is one of the oldest patterns of tarot that has stood the test of time, and it's a lot more common in France and other Francophone nations than the Rider Waite Smith cards. It is named after the city it originates from, where there were many popular decks just like it during the 1850s. This deck uses pip cards, and the minor arcana isn't represented with genre art but with regular illustrations meant to show the number of items in each suit. This could have made it harder to read if you need the visuals to help you interpret the meanings, or, on the flip side, it could be liberating for you. This deck is also used as a playing card in the Francophone regions, and it later became the root of the Thoth and Rider Waite Smith decks, created by Lady Frieda Harris and Pamela Colman Smith, respectively.

The Rider Waite Smith Tarot

This is more common with the Anglophone world, and it was Pamela Coleman Smith who first illustrated these cards, meaning to use them strictly for occult and esoteric matters. This deck has a richly illustrated minor arcana, making it excellent for divination. It was first published in 1909, and it had a companion book entitled

The Pictorial Key to the Tarot, written by A. E. Waite. This book offered the interpretations of the cards we still use to this day.

Coleman and Waite were part of a metaphysical society called the Golden Dawn, and this society firmly believed in working with the tarot in a larger context of various esoteric ideas. The Rider Waite Smith deck was crafted specifically to avoid being tied to kabbalistic and astrological matters. It was supposed to be mass-produced for the average person, and the last thing they wanted was to turn people off by having a connection to such esoteric matters. Therefore, the images on the cards were drawn from a collection of visions that Smith had conceived.

The Thoth Tarot

The illustrations on the Thoth deck were created by Lady Frieda Harris, a student of the late, great Aleister Crowley, a highly prolific and equally controversial master of the occult and was also the founder of Thelema. Frieda had offered to make a new form of tarot inspired by Crowley's Book of Law. So, they worked together for 5 years to develop the Thoth tarot deck, but neither of them lived long enough to witness its publication. It's different from the Rider Waite Smith deck because it doesn't shy away from using esoteric images and chooses to use visuals that have relatable narratives, with references to alchemy and the Kabbalah.

Correspondences between These Three Decks

There are many differences between these decks, but it's neither easy nor practical to attempt to cover every nuanced difference between them. However, we will go over the basics to work from there on your own. Note that for the purpose of this book, we'll be working with and referring to the Rider Waite Smith deck.

Differences in Minor Arcana Names

Rider Waite Smith: Wands, Cups, Swords, Pentacles

Marseille: Batons, Cups, Swords, Coins

Thoth: Wands, Cups, Swords, Disks

Differences in Court Card Names

Rider Waite Smith: Page, Knight, Queen, King

Marseille: Page, knife, Queen, King

Thoth: Princess, Prince, Queen, Knight

Differences in Major Arcana Names

Note that some of the following cards are equal to others but ordered differently, and this is why I include the numbers of each card, so there's no confusion. I'll begin by listing the cards in one deck before moving on to another, and you can match them in order of how they're listed.

Rider Waite Smith

0.Fool
1.Magician.
2.High Priestess.
3.Empress.
4.Emperor.
5.Hierophant.
6.Lovers.
7.Chariot
8.Strength.
9.Hermit.
10.Wheel of Fortune.
11.Justice.
12.Hanged Man.
13.Death.
14.Temperance.
15.Devil.

16.Tower.

17.Star.

18.Moon.

19.Sun.

20.Judgment.

21.World.

Marseilles

Le Mat/Fool (this card has no number).

0. Le Bateleur or Juggler.

1. 2. La Papesse or Popess.

2. L'imperatrice or Empress.

3. L'Empereur or Emperor.

4. Le Pape or Pope.

5. L'Amoureux or Lovers.

6. Le Chariot or Chariot.

7. La Force or Strength.

8. L'Ermite or Hermit.

9. La Roue de Fortune or Wheel of Fortune.

10. La Justice or Justice.

11. Le Pendu or Hanged Man.

12. (Unnamed)

13. Temperance or Temperance.

14. Le Diable or Devil.

15. La Maison Dieu or House of God.

16. L'Etoile or Star.

17. La Lune or Moon.

18. Le Soleil or Sun.

19. Le Jugement or Judgement.

20. Le Monde or World.

Thoth

0. Fool.

1. Magus.

2. High Priestess.

3. Empress.

4. Emperor.

5. Hierophant.

6. Lovers.

7. Chariot.

8. Lust.

9. Hermit.

10. Fortune.

11. Adjustment.

12. Hanged man.

13. Death.

14. Art.

15. Devil.

16. Tower.

17. Star.

18. Moon.

19. Sun.

20. Aeon.

21. Universe.

Choosing the Right Deck

To pick the right deck, you'll need to tap into your intuition. Hold the boxes, feel them, and ask the sellers if they have samples you can really take a look at. Often, the store owners will have samples you can take a closer look at, as long as it's a local store and not one of the larger chains. You could also talk to any friends or people on forums to find out which decks they like best and why, so you can figure out what works best for you.

As you look at the various decks available, pay attention to those that continue to call out to you. If you notice you keep picking up a certain deck, this may be the one you should use.

Some people say you should make your own deck instead of buying one. However, there's no rule regarding this. You can buy a deck if you want to, and there will be no bad juju or repercussions to deal with if you choose to buy one. It will work just as well or even better than one someone gave you or used before. Also, make sure you're getting a deck with the complete set of cards. In other words, go for the traditional deck with 78 cards. Note that choosing wisdom cards or oracle decks might not be the best choice because they may not align with the Tarot teachings you'll learn.

The Rider Waite Smith deck is a wonderful option if you are confused about what to get. It may not be the most aesthetically pleasing, but it's the most commonly used one – and it's the easiest to begin with. As you get better at working with these and learning their meanings, feel free to start using newer decks.

Chapter 2: How Astrology Enhances Tarot

Astrology is common these days. It's a cosmic art that helps you understand why you act the way you do and the best way to navigate your life based on the positions of the heavenly bodies when you were born.

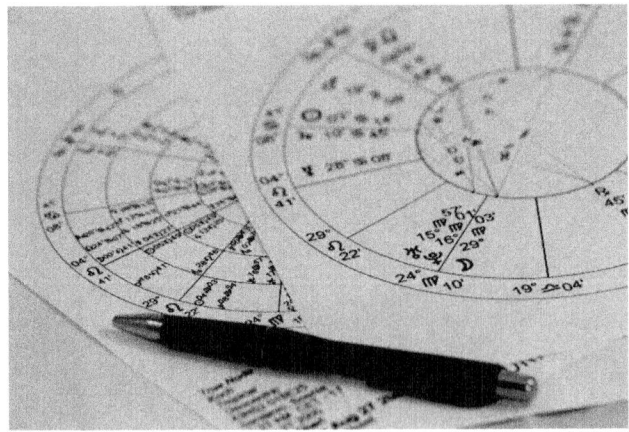

The Hermetic principle "as above, so below" is about all things in the physical world coming first from the spiritual realm, or the world of mind and thought. However, that could be applied to astrology, too, as we look to the stars above to learn what's going on in our lives on this Earth.

It's only natural to seek to understand who we are and why we're here. We've always looked up to the stars, wondering what they know about our past and our true origins, trying to figure out our present lives and what the future holds for us. Up until the 18th century, astronomy and astrology were both deeply connected. The natural dance of the sun, moon, and stars offers us a blueprint for life and living here on Earth. However, the more modern we became, the better we got at keeping the lights on when the natural sunlight was out, the easier it became to forget to look up at the sky. However, astrology is still very relevant today and can tell us a lot about our path in life.

There are several systems and schools of thought in astrology. One point of view holds that the stars and planets in the sky act as a mirror of our lives on earth. The positions of these heavenly bodies and how they move can help us know what our place and purpose are. The language of the stars is rich with imagination, offering clarity, perspective, and deep, profound insights into how we feel, what we believe, and how we act.

Fears and Myths

The more popular astrology gets, the more myths and fears come up surrounding the subject. To be clear, astrology is not a system of belief. Nor is it a cult or a religion. It's not something you need to be afraid of either, because it's only a tool and nothing more.

Some think that astrology is inaccurate. They don't know any better because they have only learned about the basic sun signs. They know nothing about the other aspects of astrology that can offer a better perspective on people's personalities and lives. If you've ever assumed there's no reason to take astrology seriously, by the time we tell you about moon signs and more, you'll see things differently.

Tarot and Astrology: A Match Made in Heaven

Tarot and astrology go together wonderfully well. Astrology offers structure, while tarot is more fluid and lends itself to interpretations based on intuition. Astrology is about analyzing, calculating, and interpreting the planets and stars using empiricism, while tarot is conceptual art.

Tarot is often considered a prime system for seeking wisdom because of its sheer diversity and because it considers other magical systems, symbolism, and esoteric concepts.

The tarot's major arcana corresponds with the zodiac's planets, moons, and stars. No one knows who originally figured out the correlation between the two, but these correspondences have existed for centuries and have proven themselves to be valuable and valid.

Different experts have assigned different astral elements to the trump cards of the tarot based on their own insight and experiences, but you shouldn't let this deter you from combining astrology and tarot. Combining these two systems is a potent oracle and combining them together will give your divination readings even more accuracy and depth. However, some of the zodiacal characteristics may not fit in easily with the personality of the Trumps, or they may not fit in easily with your spread. Whenever you find yourself confused by these conflicting juxtapositions, you should take your time to feel through them. If you notice that the zodiac signifier and major arcana are confounding, it may be that your right brain and left brain are arguing it out. In other words, your logical side and intuitive side are duking it out. Allow them to work it out and then relax. In fact, step away from the matter for a while.

There's a very high chance that when you give yourself time to figure it out without forcing it, you will find that these two views will click wonderfully. The trick is not to force yourself to see the meaning but to allow the meaning to come to you. When they show up, you'll come to powerful conclusions that you can use to change your life for the better.

Your horoscope is the map of your life based on your birth date and time. The ones you get every month let you know what you should expect for the month. Usually, to learn about what the planets are up to and how long they will radiate energy, you look at the ephemeris, which is basically a table that lets you know where each planet will be, what their aspects are, and what changes you can expect depending on your zodiac sign.

For instance, you can learn the timing of events you anticipate in your life by looking at the sign related to your tarot. For instance, you may wonder when you're going to get a raise and whether you'll get the tarot card connected to Sagittarius. As Sagittarius is in the months of November and December, it could mean you'd have to wait until that time to apply for a raise. Now, assume the card you drew isn't connected to a zodiac sign, but a planet – and the planet in question is Jupiter. It could then mean that the astrological aspect of this planet will be more critical to the time you can or will get a raise. This is how tarot and astrology can intersect with one another. As you can see, it's pretty easy to understand when you get the hang of it.

Deeper Relationships

One thing you should look for first is the card's elements, as they will let you know which astrological sign group you're dealing with. Zodiac signs are either earth, water, fire, or air signs, and you can tell what you're dealing with just by looking at the card.

Also, when you consider the energy of the elements, you'll find they're connected with the tarot suits. For instance, the Cups suit is clearly related to the water signs: Pisces, Scorpio, and Cancer. The Swords suit is connected to the air signs, Libra, Gemini, and Aquarius. The Wand suit is connected to Sagittarius, Leo, and Aries, which are fire signs. The Earth signs are Virgo, Taurus, and Capricorn, and they are connected to the Pentacles Suit.

You can still dive deeper into each sign and its relationship with the tarot cards. Here's what you need to know to do that:

- **Aries**: 2, 3, and 4 of the Wand suit.
- **Taurus**: 5, 6, and 7 of the Pentacles suit.
- **Gemini**: 8, 9, and 10 of the Swords suit.
- **Cancer**: 2, 3, and 4 of the Cups suit.
- **Leo**: 5, 6, and 7 of the Wand suit.
- **Virgo**: 8, 9, and 10 of the Pentacles suit.
- **Libra**: 2, 3, and 4 of the Swords suit.
- **Scorpio**: 5, 6, and 7 of the Cups suit.
- **Sagittarius**: 8, 9, and 10 of the Wand suit.
- **Capricorn**: 2, 3, and 4 of the Pentacles suit.
- **Aquarius**: 5, 6, and 7 of the Swords suit.
- **Pisces**: 8, 9, and 10 of the Cups suit.

Putting together all of this information, you can see how astrology and the tarot can come together to create very powerful readings. You'll be able to gain even more insight into your horoscope when you work with tarot at the same time.

Correspondences

Now let's go over the correspondences between the Trumps and their zodiacal and planetary counterparts.

Fool: Uranus. Its traits are new ideas, experimentation, and modern thought.

Magician: Mercury. Its traits are transformation, understanding, connection, and relationship.

Priestess: Moon. The traits are subconscious thoughts, intuition, moods, and sensitivity.

Empress: Venus. The traits are refinement, pleasure, poetry, music, art, love, beauty.

Emperor: Aries. These traits are ambition, effectiveness, determination, demand, and being active.

Hierophant: Taurus. Its traits are patience, instruction, appreciation, subtle strength, and security.

Lovers: Gemini. Its traits are changeability, intelligence, inquisitiveness, and communication.

Chariot: Cancer. The traits here are impulsivity, intensity, diplomacy, and emotion.

Strength: Leo. The traits are compassion, initiative, faithfulness, power, warmth, and ruling.

Hermit: Virgo. The traits are thoughtfulness, observation, reflectiveness, practicality, and analysis.

Wheel: Jupiter. The traits are receptivity, expansion, good fortune, hope, enthusiasm.

Justice: Libra. The traits are perfection, beauty, truth, justice, and balance.

Hanged Man: Neptune. The traits are distortion, psychic, idealism, imagination, and illusion.

Death: Scorpio. This is related to isolation, unyielding, purposefulness, self-will, and transience.

Temperance: Sagittarius. This is related to optimism, experimentation, motion, and philosophy.

Devil: Capricorn. This is connected to traits like willfulness, practicality, preservation, dominance, and determination.

Tower: Mars. This is connected to traits like assertion, energy, courage, intensity, and facilitation.

Star: Aquarius. This is tied to duplicity, insight, seriousness, humanitarianism, and knowledge.

Moon: Pisces. This has traits like perception, reactivity, imagination, depth, and fluctuation.

Sun: Sun. This is connected to identity, will, creativity, vitality, energy, and focus.

Judgment: Pluto. This is tied to realization, experience, improvement, enlightenment, and perspective.

World: Saturn. The traits associated are patience, depth, accomplishment, discipline, and concentration.

When you start to get used to the connections between astrology and tarot, and you think about the correlations I've offered here, you will begin to notice a much deeper relationship with each of the cards of the major arcana. If you want to better understand life, you should regularly work with these two systems and incorporate them into your readings. That way, your readings become instinctive based on the knowledge you have gained.

Numerology and Tarot

When looking at tarot cards, most readers tend to ignore the significance of the numbers on the cards, which is a shame. There is a lot of symbolism with each card, and the numbers shouldn't be dismissed as being anything more than a tool to catalog the cards. They can help you delve even deeper into the mystical. If you want to understand a card's energy, you should look at everything about the card, including the numbers.

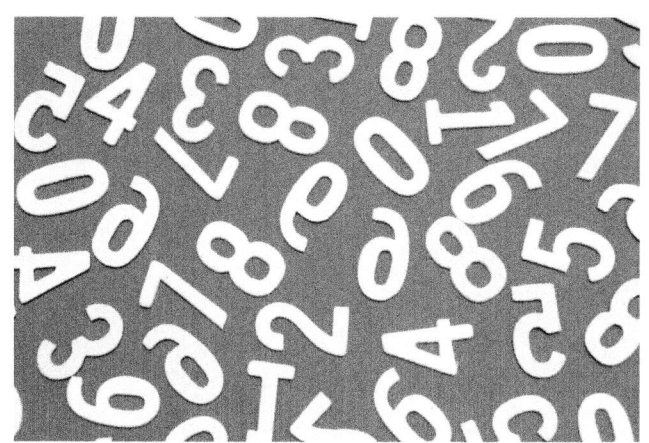

Numbers have their own vibrations, which affect us all. Their vibrations resonate with energies of the same frequency throughout the whole universe. So, when you take a look at a tarot spread and factor in the numbers, you can glean a lot of information from using the vibrations of the numbers to add further nuanced meaning to the readings from the cards. The meanings of these numbers can lead to oracles in the form of geometry and symmetry, and they can bring you incredible accuracy in your reading. Numerology is the study of numbers and how they affect how we live. It's seeing life through the framework of numbers and their vibrations.

Another factor you need to consider is whether the signs are mutable, fixed, or cardinal. These are the *modalities* of the signs. Mutable signs are flexible and changeable, fixed signs are unmovable and stubborn, while cardinal signs are leaders and initiators.

The numbers of the cards that line up with the zodiac signs can tell you a lot. For instance, when you look at the suits with cards with 2, 3, or 4 on them, those are cardinal signs: Capricorn, Libra, Cancer, and Aries.

When you see the numbers 5, 6, or 7, these are fixed signs: Aquarius, Leo, Scorpio, and Taurus. These signs aren't easy to budge or nudge along if you want them to move in a certain direction or at a faster pace.

Finally, you have the mutable signs, Virgo, Pisces, Gemini, and Sagittarius, who are the sort of people willing to go with the flow. They are adventurous and spontaneous, easy to be around and have fun with. The numbers in question here are 8, 9, and 10.

When it comes to tarot numerology, you have to reduce the numbers to the lowest, single digit. For instance, if the card you draw is Temperance, a number 14 card, you have to reduce the number 14 by adding each digit to get 5. Some tarot readers would rather not reduce the numbers; instead, they choose to focus on the second digit, which in our example would be 4. Whatever you choose to do, your readings will be augmented in a lovely way. You might also come to realize the paradox of the numbers, as they both create a grounding effect on your reading while making room for creativity and elasticity. The takeaway from this chapter is that you should consider the planets, stars, and numbers along with the cards you draw.

Chapter 3: The Sun, Moon, and Rising Signs

The thing about astrology is that it's not only about the sun signs, although this is all many people tend to focus on. When you want to read someone's natal chart accurately, you have to consider the big three; their sun sign, moon sign, and rising sign.

What Are Sun Signs?

Sun signs are the easiest aspect of astrology for people to understand, and many books and websites only list sun sign information. While there is some reliable info out there about sun signs, that's all it is: basic information. To get a good idea of someone's personality, you need more than just their sun sign–you need their moon and rising signs as well. The whole concept of astrology is based on the position of the Sun, Moon, and all the planets at the exact time we were born (the moment we got stuck with our terrible personalities).

In astrology, a sun sign is one's position in society based on the zodiac. In other words, it refers to what time of year people were born. Each person falls into one of twelve sun signs:

- **Aries** - March 21 to April 19
- **Taurus** - April 20 to May 20
- **Gemini** - May 21 to June 21
- **Cancer** - June 22 to July 22
- **Leo** - July 23 to August 22
- **Virgo** - August 23 to September 22
- **Libra** - September 23 to October 22
- **Scorpio** - October 23 to November 22
- **Sagittarius** - November 23 to December 21
- **Capricorn** - December 22 to January 20
- **Aquarius** - January 21 to February 18
- **Pisces** - February 19 to March 20

Sun signs are very important when it comes to studying astrology. They help define a certain set of qualities assigned by the stars at birth, including being silly or outgoing, hardworking or lazy, and so on. However, there are always exceptions. It is up to the individual how they take advantage of their sign and what they make out of it.

Misunderstandings about Sun Signs

The sun sign is the most commonly used form of astrological delineation. People who have just discovered a love for astrology may immediately ask which sun sign they belong to when learning about the zodiac. Sun signs are popular because people can learn a lot about their personalities and character from them. However, there are so many misunderstandings about these signs that it's important to know what sun signs mean before you read too far into your own or someone else's chart.

One common misconception is that everyone born under one particular sun sign has the same personality. This is untrue for many reasons, starting with the fact that astrologers don't agree on what sun sign personalities are supposed to be like anyway. The twelve signs of the zodiac are divided into four elements: fire, earth, air, and water. Each element has three qualities: cardinal (new beginnings), fixed (stable), and mutable (adaptable). There are a total of twelve possible combinations. While some generalizations can be made about each sign and its element and quality according to the Western tradition, there is no uniform consensus about which characteristics belong to which sun sign.

A second misunderstanding is that your sun sign represents your most dominant traits or most defining characteristics as an individual human being. It doesn't. It represents the sign in which the Sun was present on your day of birth. The sun is one small part of your astrological chart; it's not like everything else doesn't matter. The information the rest of your chart provides just as much bearing on how others perceive you and how you see yourself.

Thirdly, there is no such thing as "the best" sun sign for every situation. How often have you heard people say things like, "I'm so glad I got invited to this Gemini party because they always know how to have fun."? Or "I'm so glad my child was born under Cancer because they're such nurturing and caring people." Sun sign analysis suggests that different signs are more advantageous than others for specific types of interactions. This idea of the best sun sign is just plain silly and can lead to problems when someone with a supposedly "lesser" sun sign tries to compete with these so-called superstars. The truth is that everyone has their own strengths and weaknesses.

Don't get discouraged if you don't fit traditional ideas about your sun sign. Even if there were some solid evidence proving what your personality is like based on where the Sun was on your day of birth, it's still not going to tell you everything about who you are as a person. Sun signs are just one small part of the big picture that is your astrological chart.

Don't let yourself be put off by sun sign misinformation when you do further reading and research about astrology, either. You may find things like, "Geminis should really look at their Cancer moon," or, "Cancers can get along better with Taurus than they can with Gemini." The truth is every human being alive has a different set of strengths and weaknesses. We find ourselves in vastly different situations on a daily basis. If there such a thing as the best sun sign for every situation, everyone would end up the same way; successful and happy.

Aries (March 21-April 19)

Bold and brash, Aries is quick to act. They like to take the lead on projects and encourage their team members to get involved. However, if someone takes over or tries to boss them around, they will soon put a stop to it. It's important to Aries that everyone (including themselves) is given full credit for their work and achievements.

Aries

If you need your hand held, Aries will make it happen. If more hands are needed, they will not hesitate to walk over the top of whoever is in their way. They like receiving praise and recognition and can be surprisingly shy when the compliments come from someone they're keen on (or trying to impress). The Aries is all about getting things done, so if they say they're going to do something, you can count on it happening.

Aries has a lot of energy, but they tend to use up all their resources early in the day, so try not to keep them around too late. They may come across as arrogant and brash, but they're actually very sensitive and may feel hurt if you don't want to join in with their ideas. They can sometimes get carried away by their enthusiasm, so someone must be around to rein them in when needed.

They are fiercely competitive and always try new things just for the thrill of doing something different (even if they're not very good at it). They don't like being tied down with long-term commitments, so they may leave you hanging on for a change of plan.

Taurus (April 20-May 20)

Gentle yet dependable, Taurus has an unbreakable sense of loyalty. Once they let you into their inner circle, you're part of their family for life. They are also very patient, almost to a fault. You could be waiting years for Taurus to show up, but they will always arrive on time (or early).

Taurus

Taurus is very sensual and loves physical contact, so give them hugs as often as possible. If you can keep Taurus smiling, then you've already won their heart. They're emotional and easily hurt, so try not to take them for granted, or they may just do a slow burn.

They love luxury and ease, so you mustn't give them any grief if they spend lots of money on themselves. Taurus is very direct about what they want, so they prefer you to say something straight out if you need to say something. Don't expect them to read between the lines or try to solve your problems for you – let them know exactly what's on your mind if you want their support.

Gemini (May 21 - June 20)

Talkative and outgoing, Geminis are great at getting conversations going. They love discussing ideas and opinions, but they can also get bored of talking about the same thing over and over again. Geminis are easily distracted, so be mindful that sometimes it's best to let them produce their own opinion rather than force-feed them your viewpoint.

Geminis have a great sense of humor and love to laugh, so you'll always be entertained by their quirky witticisms. They are audacious and don't mind sticking their necks out for what they believe in, but they're also very good at playing devil's advocate if it means getting to the truth of an issue.

Geminis like doing things on the spur of the moment, so be prepared to change plans at a moment's notice. They hate feeling bored or trapped in one place for too long and can sometimes feel smothered if you don't give them time alone to recharge.

Cancer (June 21-July 22)

Jovial yet sensitive, Cancer takes great pleasure in looking after the people they love. They are warm and nurturing, with a good sense of adventure. Cancers might not be very forthcoming about their feelings, so it's up to you to try to figure out how they're feeling from the clues that they give you.

They have a lot of friends from all walks of life because they enjoy being inspired by other people's stories. They are very protective when it comes to the people they care about, so feel honored that they put so much faith in you. However, this also means that Cancer can be very private and won't tell you everything straight away-you'll have to earn their trust first.

Their emotions run deep, but they don't like showing vulnerability, so be gentle and patient when you're trying to get them to open up. They can be very moody if their emotions are unbalanced, so try to spot the warning signs and take care of them if they start feeling overwhelmed.

Leo (July 23-Aug. 22)

Flamboyant and self-assured, Leos always know what they want. They make great leaders because they're very passionate about the causes they believe in. Leos are also generous and don't mind sharing their resources with others, but this can sometimes reveal a bit of an ego that loves to be center stage all the time.

They love to be admired, so you must tell them how wonderful they are. They can be self-centered, so don't feel like you're not getting enough attention if you're in a relationship with them. Leos prefer to be adored rather than understood most of the time, but they also love being challenged because it makes them feel alive and motivated to grow.

Leo is ruled by the Sun, so they are very connected to its energy. They need plenty of space to feel comfortable but also enjoy being near people that make them laugh and whom they can turn to for fun and adventure.

Virgo (Aug 23-Sept 22)

Loyalty is everything to Virgos, so you'll always feel secure in their company. If you ever need anything, whether it's an ear to listen to or a helping hand, they'll be there for you without hesitation. However, Virgos can also be really hard on themselves, so try not to take their self-deprecating comments too seriously – they just want to do things perfectly.

Virgos are perfectionists and expect the same high standards from their partners, but they also like to be treated with respect and consideration. They often put other people before themselves, so make sure that you take care of them once in a while if you want them to stick around.

They may seem fussy or overly critical at times, but Virgos are governed by Mercury, the planet of communication. They hate having to repeat themselves or tell other people about their feelings, but if you try and understand them instead of getting frustrated with them, they'll appreciate it more than you know.

Libra (September 23-October 22)

Venus rules Libras, so they're naturally in tune with other people's feelings, whether they want to be or not. They have strong intuition and don't tend to do things by accident, so you can trust that their actions come from a genuine place.

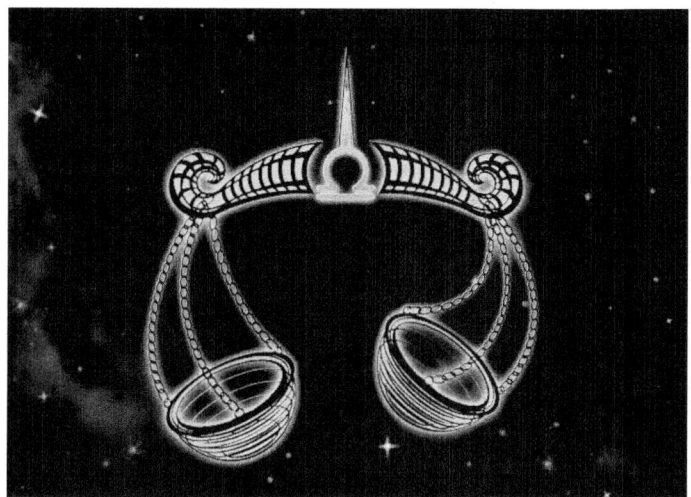

Libras are social creatures who love being around other people, but they sometimes forget about themselves. You must try and relax your Libra if they're working too hard and don't reward them for their kindness with a constant sense of urgency.

They have a very balanced approach to life, so you'll rarely see Libras get upset or angry with other people – they'd rather walk away from the fight than stay around and let negativity ruin their day. As long as you show Libras that you appreciate their input, they'll be more than happy to help you out whenever needed.

Scorpio (Oct 23-Nov 21)

Scorpios are deeply passionate people, but this can often lead them to act without thinking first, so just try your best not to get in the way of their impulsiveness. Their thirst for knowledge and desire to explore the world makes Scorpios very curious beings.

They are naturally intuitive, so you mustn't lie or cheat around them. They can see right through your tricks. If you're willing to be open with a Scorpio, they'll do whatever it takes to show you that they care about you and your well-being.

They don't do anything by halves and hate feeling like they've done something wrong, but this makes them very devoted partners once you get to know them better. Scorpios are very good at seeing past people's flaws too, which is a rare quality that should be cherished whenever it appears.

Sagittarius (November 22-December 21)

Sagittarians are cheerful people who love to share their knowledge and wisdom with others. They believe that everyone should be treated equally regardless of race, religion, gender, or sexuality, so you'll never feel judged by a Sagittarius.

Sagittarians can also come across as very blunt because they don't like wasting their breath on meaningless conversations. They would much rather get straight to the point. If you can accept a Sagittarius for who they are and understand that sometimes their way of thinking is different from yours, then they'll be one of your most loyal friends.

Sagittarians tend to idealize people, leading them to make bad choices, but once they've learned from their mistakes, they never repeat them. They're very open-minded, which can be great if you're looking for someone who will introduce you to new ideas and cultures. Do remember, though, that Sagittarians are also very independent people, so don't smother them or try to control what they do.

Capricorn (Dec 22-Jan 19)

Capricorns are very ambitious people who enjoy having a plan for their life. This may make them seem unapproachable or even cold at times, but just remember that they're willing to work hard to achieve everything that they want out of life.

Saturn rules Capricorns, the planet that represents time, so they're very practical beings who tend to think about how much effort is needed to perform a certain task. They can be quite guarded around people and take their time getting to know you, but once you've earned their respect and trust, it'll be impossible for them to let you down.

Their stubbornness means that Capricorns are happy to see something through to the end, but this also means that they're often misunderstood by people who don't know them well enough. If you want a partner who will work tirelessly to support your dreams, then look no further than a Capricorn.

Aquarius (Jan 20-Feb 18)

Aquarians are intelligent people who enjoy discussing new ideas with others. This also means that they can come across as intimidating or distant sometimes. They love to help people but always value their independence, so you'll never be able to force Aquarians to do anything they don't want to.

Aquarians are ruled by Uranus, which makes them very rebellious beings - just don't try and force your values on them, or they'll be quick to cut you out of their lives. They can also come across as cold and aloof, but this is only because Aquarians value honesty so strongly that they don't have time for anything less.

Aquarians love expressing themselves freely, so if you want a partner who will always tell you how they feel, then go for an Aquarius.

Pisces (Feb 19-Mar 20)

Pisceans are very curious people, making them seem restless or easily distracted at times. They are naturally spiritual beings with a lot of insight, so if you have problems in your life that need solving, it's essential to seek out a Piscean.

Pisceans are very compassionate and kind people, which means that they're always willing to lend a hand or give you a shoulder to cry on. As long as you can accept their need for independence, then you'll find that Pisceans make the best partners because they will never let you down once they've given their heart away.

They can be shy around people, so it may take them some time before they start opening up about themselves, but once they do, you'll quickly realize why so many people love being around Pisceans-they truly are beautiful beings who deserve to have the world handed to them on a plate.

What Do the Moon Signs Mean?

Your moon sign is based upon the exact time you were born, which differs from your sun sign. It's where the moon was when you were born. You can find out what your moon sign - or other non-sun signs - are by using an astrological tool called a birth chart or natal chart.

In astrology, a moon sign is one of twelve equal divisions of the zodiac that fall along the ecliptic between your sun and ascendant. The placement of planets in these thirty-degree sections reveals certain personality traits and life circumstances. Each section spans roughly seven days, with a new moon beginning a new lunar cycle every twenty-nine and a half days. As such, no two people with the same birthday share the same individual moon sign.

The moon rules your emotions. It also gives insight into your daily routine and how you feel when you are at home or with family. If you have a lot of planets/points in water signs (Cancer, Scorpio, and Pisces), then this is an indication of being very emotional. Planets in fire signs (Leo, Aries, and Sagittarius) indicate being more high-strung or having nervous energy. Although it has nothing to do with the phase of the moon, if any planet falls within 8 degrees of the moon, it will affect your emotions.

Your moon sign is very important because it reflects the subconscious and hidden part of you that you don't show others. It's what shapes your soul and your feelings, reflecting your deepest desires and needs and what makes you feel secure. It's the part you hide from others, but when people know your moon placement, they'll know how to treat you and meet your deepest needs.

The moon sign, phase, and house tell you plenty about your emotional habits and instincts. Knowing this can help you develop emotionally, express your subconscious habits, and shed light on why you do the things you do. It can also affect the strength of the expression of your sun sign. Suppose you're a fiery Leo with a gentle Taurus moon. You may find your aggression reduced by the mellow effect of Taurus. Also, if you're a Pisces with a Scorpio moon, you can have amazing intuition and be extra emotional. This moon sign is why people of the same sun sign express themselves differently. The moon sign is the expression of who you are behind closed doors, the one who comes up when you're unguarded and have to act when you're in the middle of a crisis.

Moon in Aries: You have a pioneering spirit, making you want to lead a life full of adventure and excitement. Your boldness can often seem foolhardy to others, but you would rather blaze a trail than sit back and wait for someone else to pave it for you. You are also very restless – nothing pleases you more than starting something new – but your tendency to get bored quickly can make you fickle at times. In relationships, this position of Mars indicates that the person has a strong sex drive but may tend to get into many short-term relationships.

Moon in Taurus: You are the quintessential homebody who craves security and stability above all else. You are highly sensual, which makes you enjoy having fun with your significant other. However, you are so set in your ways that it can be difficult for anyone to change them. People born under this moon sign require their own space to retreat to once in a while. Borderline materialistic, you also tend to be possessive about your belongings.

Moon in Gemini: This Moon position indicates that you enjoy variety more than most people. You crave new experiences because they feed your never-ending curiosity about life. As a result, you may often find yourself in a whirlwind of activities that can leave you feeling scattered and exhausted. However, your intellectual skills are well-honed to the point where communication comes very easily for you.

Moon in Cancer: The Moon is in its own sign here, which indicates that the person can be highly sensitive and intuitive. You crave deep emotional connections with others more than most people do, but you may lack true depth in your relationships because of your fear of getting hurt or taking on responsibilities (because if you did get hurt or have to take on responsibility, it would only be because you let down some of your guard). A bit moody at times but also quite nurturing, this position of Mars makes for great parenting skills. If things come up that need to be discussed, don't be afraid to talk about them with your partner.

Moon in Leo: You have a strong desire to lead others, which can be both helpful and problematic. You are very creative, so you may find yourself taking on many different projects simultaneously, but your tendency to scatter your energy means that you will not complete most of these tasks. Your warmth and vitality make you one of the most heart-centered people around, as well as one of the most loving. But this position can indicate possible problems with fertility (or lack thereof).

Moon in Virgo: This sign indicates workaholics who take their responsibilities quite seriously. You sometimes lack flexibility; you need to keep an open mind and learn how to lighten up every once in a while. You are very dedicated to your careers, so much so that you have a hard time separating work life from personal life. People with this moon sign often find themselves in relationships where they need the other person just as much as the other person wants or needs them.

Moon in Libra: The Moon is in its own sign here, which indicates that you can be emotionally balanced and forgiving. Because of your innate sense of fairness, you often feel compelled to take care of others, even if it hampers your own happiness. This makes for great relationships but can also make you over-extend yourself at times. However, one great quality about this position on Mars is that it gives you excellent intuitive skills, so use them.

You are very intense when it comes to relationships because this position of Mars makes you highly sexual, which also means that you may have a hard time getting physically intimate with someone who doesn't live up to your expectations. However, if the other person is right for you, they will be able to handle your somewhat possessive nature and fiery passion. People born under this moon sign tend to be highly intuitive, but they may sometimes go overboard and start reading into things too much (which can lead to miscommunications).

Moon in Sagittarius: This position gives you the ability to perceive life through a spiritual lens. You make excellent teachers and counselors. However, people born under this moon sign should avoid spreading themselves too thin because of their love for travel and learning. You are also very open-minded. Don't be afraid to show it at times (don't get so caught up in your reactions that you forget how to respond).

Moon in Capricorn: The Moon is in its own sign here, which indicates that you have a deeply ingrained sense of ambition. With this position, Mars, you tend to build things up only to tear them down just as quickly. Your life can become rather impulsive because of this, but fortunately, the people around you will forgive your mistakes because they know your heart is always in the right place. You may not always realize it, but others look up to you for guidance. When the time is right, do what you can for them.

Moon in Aquarius: You have a hard time being present in a relationship because your mind is always on something else. But this position of Mars gives you an admirable sense of social justice, so try to channel that energy into your romantic life. Your need for freedom tends to either attract or repel people depending on their compatibility with you, so it's sometimes best if you wait until things are serious before making connections (don't be afraid to get out there and date, though.).

Moon in Pisces: You have extreme emotional highs and lows with this moon sign, but these fluctuations can actually bring balance to your relationships. It's also harder for you than others to speak up about what you want; try to be more assertive. Sometimes, you find yourself attracted to people who are out of your reach; don't let the fact that they are unattainable scare you. A person with this moon sign can easily fall in love with someone's mind, so take time to get to know someone before jumping right into things.

What Are the Rising Signs?

Rising signs are also called "ascendant" or "Asc" signs. They refer to the signs that ascend towards the east when people are born. Similar to sun sign astrology, moon sign astrology focuses on how the moon behaves when you're born instead of how it behaves in general.

Ascendant Signs are known as the "personality" of a person's zodiac sign, which are the twelve constellations on the ecliptic. They are also simply known as "Rising." The Ascendant is what you seem to be on the outside. It is not your physical appearance but how others might perceive you. Ascendant signs are the first impression of one's personality and can tell you a lot about yourself. Dealing with other people is like walking into a crowded room full of strangers, but if you know which sign each person has, it makes it easier to make quick assumptions about who they are and therefore connects with them better. You can draw conclusions about what they are like, their strengths and weaknesses, hobbies, likes and dislikes, and so on.

To calculate your rising sign, it's best to seek the help of an astrologer, who will help you figure it out using your birth date and time, as well as the location you were born in. You need to know the hour of your birth and your sun sign, but if you're not sure, you can use online calculators for free to figure out your rising sign. Some of these calculators have an option you can check if you don't know your birth time. Here's a general guide for getting your rising sign:

Aries

- 6 AM to 8 AM – Taurus
- 8 AM to 10 AM – Gemini
- 10 AM to 12 PM – Cancer
- 12 PM to 2 PM – Leo
- 2 PM to 4 PM – Virgo

- 4 PM to 6 PM – Libra
- 6 PM to 8 PM – Scorpio
- 8 PM to 10 PM – Sagittarius
- 10 PM to 12 AM – Capricorn
- 12 AM to 2 AM – Aquarius
- 2 AM to 4 AM – Pisces
- 4 AM to 6 AM – Aries

Taurus

- 6 AM to 8 AM – Gemini
- 8 AM to 10 AM – Cancer
- 10 AM to 12 PM – Leo
- 12 PM to 2 PM – Virgo
- 2 PM to 4 PM – Libra
- 4 PM to 6 PM – Scorpio
- 6 PM to 8 PM – Sagittarius
- 8 PM to 10 PM – Capricorn
- 10 PM to 12 AM – Aquarius
- 12 AM to 2 AM – Pisces
- 2 AM to 4 AM – Aries
- 4 AM to 6 AM – Taurus

Gemini

- 6 AM to 8 AM – Cancer
- 8 AM to 10 AM – Leo
- 10 AM to 12 PM – Virgo
- 12 PM to 2 PM – Libra
- 2 PM to 4 PM – Scorpio
- 4 PM to 6 PM – Sagittarius
- 6 PM to 8 PM – Capricorn
- 8 PM to 10 PM – Aquarius
- 10 PM to 12 AM – Pisces

- 12 AM to 2 AM – Aries
- 2 AM to 4 AM – Taurus
- 4 AM to 6 AM – Gemini

Cancer

- 6 AM to 8 AM – Leo
- 8 AM to 10 AM – Virgo
- 10 AM to 12 PM – Libra
- 12 PM to 2 PM – Scorpio
- 2 PM to 4 PM – Sagittarius
- 4 PM to 6 PM – Capricorn
- 6 PM to 8 PM – Aquarius
- 8 PM to 10 PM – Pisces
- 10 PM to 12 AM – Aries
- 12 AM to 2 AM – Taurus
- 2 AM to 4 AM – Gemini
- 4 AM to 6 AM – Cancer

Leo

- 6 AM to 8 AM – Virgo
- 8 AM to 10 AM – Libra
- 10 AM to 12 PM – Scorpio
- 12 PM to 2 PM – Sagittarius
- 2 PM to 4 PM – Capricorn
- 4 PM to 6 PM – Aquarius
- 6 PM to 8 PM – Pisces
- 8 PM to 10 PM – Aries
- 10 PM to 12 AM – Taurus
- 12 AM to 2 AM – Gemini
- 2 AM to 4 AM – Cancer
- 4 AM to 6 AM – Leo

Virgo

- 6 AM to 8 AM - Libra
- 8 AM to 10 AM - Scorpio
- 10 AM to 12 PM - Sagittarius
- 12 PM to 2 PM - Capricorn
- 2 PM to 4 PM - Aquarius
- 4 PM to 6 PM - Pisces
- 6 PM to 8 PM - Aries
- 8 PM to 10 PM - Taurus
- 10 PM to 12 AM - Gemini
- 12 AM to 2 AM - Cancer
- 2 AM to 4 AM - Leo
- 4 AM to 6 AM - Virgo

Libra

- 6 AM to 8 AM - Scorpio
- 8 AM to 10 AM - Sagittarius
- 10 AM to 12 PM - Capricorn
- 12 PM to 2 PM - Aquarius
- 2 PM to 4 PM - Pisces
- 4 PM to 6 PM - Aries
- 6 PM to 8 PM - Taurus
- 8 PM to 10 PM - Gemini
- 10 PM to 12 AM - Cancer
- 12 AM to 2 AM - Leo
- 2 AM to 4 AM - Virgo
- 4 AM to 6 AM - Libra

Scorpio

- 6 AM to 8 AM - Sagittarius
- 8 AM to 10 AM - Capricorn
- 10 AM to 12 PM - Aquarius

- 12 PM to 2 PM – Pisces
- 2 PM to 4 PM – Aries
- 4 PM to 6 PM – Taurus
- 6 PM to 8 PM – Gemini
- 8 PM to 10 PM – Cancer
- 10 PM to 12 AM – Leo
- 12 AM to 2 AM – Virgo
- 2 AM to 4 AM – Libra
- 4 AM to 6 AM – Scorpio

Sagittarius

- 6 AM to 8 AM – Capricorn
- 8 AM to 10 AM – Aquarius
- 10 AM to 12 PM – Pisces
- 12 PM to 2 PM – Aries
- 2 PM to 4 PM – Taurus
- 4 PM to 6 PM – Gemini
- 6 PM to 8 PM – Cancer
- 8 PM to 10 PM – Leo
- 10 PM to 12 AM – Virgo
- 12 AM to 2 AM – Libra
- 2 AM to 4 AM – Scorpio
- 4 AM to 6 AM – Sagittarius

Capricorn

- 6 AM to 8 AM – Aquarius
- 8 AM to 10 AM – Pisces
- 10 AM to 12 PM – Aries
- 12 PM to 2 PM – Taurus
- 2 PM to 4 PM – Gemini
- 4 PM to 6 PM – Cancer
- 6 PM to 8 PM – Leo

- 8 PM to 10 PM – Virgo
- 10 PM to 12 AM – Libra
- 12 AM to 2 AM – Scorpio
- 2 AM to 4 AM – Sagittarius
- 4 AM to 6 AM – Capricorn

Aquarius

- 6 AM to 8 AM – Pisces
- 8 AM to 10 AM – Aries
- 10 AM to 12 PM – Taurus
- 12 PM to 2 PM – Gemini
- 2 PM to 4 PM – Cancer
- 4 PM to 6 PM – Leo
- 6 PM to 8 PM – Virgo
- 8 PM to 10 PM – Libra
- 10 PM to 12 AM – Scorpio
- 12 AM to 2 AM – Sagittarius
- 2 AM to 4 AM – Capricorn
- 4 AM to 6 AM – Aquarius

Pisces

- 6 AM to 8 AM – Aries
- 8 AM to 10 AM – Taurus
- 10 AM to 12 PM – Gemini
- 12 PM to 2 PM – Cancer
- 2 PM to 4 PM – Leo
- 4 PM to 6 PM – Virgo
- 6 PM to 8 PM – Libra
- 8 PM to 10 PM – Scorpio
- 10 PM to 12 AM – Sagittarius
- 12 AM to 2 AM – Capricorn
- 2 AM to 4 AM – Aquarius

- 4 AM to 6 AM – Pisces

Aries Rising

People with Aries as their ascending sign are often stereotyped as being impulsive, impatient risk-takers who live life in the fast lane. This is because, when it comes to decision-making and problem-solving (which is all about taking risks), for many people, this sign does not mean they do not think things through very carefully before taking action. At its best, though, an Aries Ascendant can be courageous and pioneering. They get things done, and we call them trailblazers. Many CEOs are Aries ascendants, meaning this is definitely not a slow-paced kind of job. People with Aries Ascendants tend to be forthright and candid – very straightforward, which can lead to conflict if they are tactless or brusque. They work best in competitive situations where they can "win."

Taurus Rising

People born with Taurus as their ascending sign are known for their dependability. The bull is the classic worker bee who gets things done methodically and thoroughly. You'll always know what you're getting with this person, and they are not likely to surprise you. The Taurus Ascendant is also known for loyalty, a quality that earns them lasting friendships and true love relationships. However, they are not "touchy-feely" people, and they detest cuddling and other signs of overt affection. Do not expect an excess of laughter from a person with Taurus as their ascendant sign – the sign itself doesn't actually consider any humor particularly amusing.

Gemini Rising

The quick wit and multiple intellectual interests associated with Gemini as the ascendant make this person popular and highly intelligent. People with this sign as their ascending sign make great conversationalists, which is why it's an appealing kind of rising sign to have – it makes socializing fun. Just don't expect them to waste time on relationships or anything that requires commitment. Gemini is the polar opposite of Taurus – the bull represents reliability, while Gemini is flighty, changeable, and fickle. Gemini Ascendants are charming, but they can be arrogant, impatient, and superficial at times too.

Cancer Rising

People who have Cancer as their ascending sign are often very protective of those they love, which is a highly commendable quality. These people make excellent parents, and they tend to be good at nurturing others who need help or care. Cancer Ascendants make great counselors – they have a strong sense of empathy and an innate ability to understand others' predicaments. However, "emotional" is the word that best describes a Cancer Rising, and people with this sign as their ascendant tend to be temperamental and moody, with mercurial emotional states.

Leo Rising

People born with Leo as their ascending sign are often impressive and ambitious – they aim high in life. They love being the center of attention too, which suggests that they may have a talent for public speaking. The downside to having a Leo ascendant is that these people aren't very good listeners. They're frequently so busy talking about themselves that they don't hear what others say. For a Leo ascendant, everything is about "me." Pride is another characteristic of this sign – they tend to think much higher of themselves than others do.

Virgo Rising

People born with Virgo as their ascendant are known for being extremely fastidious and particular. They hate getting dirty or breaking the rules, which means this subject can be a bit of a stickler regarding how things should be done. In fact, they're probably reading this article from beginning to end without skipping even one word. If you have Virgo rising, you may want to do some editing before showing your friends or family – not everyone will understand how important precision is to you. People with Virgo Ascending also tend to be excellent at analyzing and logically categorizing information – they make great scientists and researchers.

Sagittarius Rising

Sagittarius, or "The Archer," was named after the mythological centaur, Sagittarius. The symbol for Sagittarius is an arrow piercing a target. This image implies that when someone who has Sagittarius ascending wants something, they aim for it and go for it no matter what. In addition to being adventurous and outgoing, Sagittarians also have a natural knack for learning new things. They are great at taking in information from books or their surroundings and organizing it in a way that makes sense to them.

However, because they have such a shooting-star quality about them, they often move around so much that they never seem to stick with anything for very long. Sagittarians also have wandering souls and can often be found traveling far from home.

Because of their wanderlust and sometimes rebellious nature, Sagittarius is a sign that is strongly associated with following one's own path in life. They aren't afraid to break away from the crowd and carve out new trails for themselves whenever they feel like it. When someone has Sagittarius ascending, there is always something exciting going on. Someone who has this placement will never find themselves bored because trouble just seems to follow them everywhere they go. Even though people born under this sign don't usually attract bad luck, they certainly know how to live an adventurous life.

Pisces Rising

Pisces rising people are often very sensitive and prefer to avoid conflict. They can be quite shy, and sometimes they let their feelings control them. Pisceans tend to be very emotional, so they rely on those around them for support and reassurance. Pisces rising people love anything that is exotic or off the beaten track as it allows them to explore new territories where nobody knows who they really are. Pisceans do not go into politics or teaching because of their dependency on others; they might also struggle with authority figures due to their flexible nature and need for freedom (remember the fish swimming in the ocean).

Pisces rising subjects often have a hard time accepting defeat. Therefore, success is often the result of their hard work. This sign loves to explore all aspects of love and hates being alone. Pisces rising people tend to have a lot of mood swings, which can be quite taxing for loved ones. However, this might come across as silliness. They are very creative individuals who make excellent actors, dancers, or musicians.

Aquarius Rising

Aquarius has Saturn as its ruling sign, so people with this rising sign tend to have a serious, driven quality to them. They're usually ahead of their time in regard to fashion and technology. That driven nature makes many Aquarians into great scientists or technical wizards because it forces them to obsess over details. They usually need to invent something or figure something out because it helps them puzzle the world together. They're very smart people who can seem quietly brilliant, but they don't think about things that aren't interesting to them most of the time. Natives born with Aquarius rising are also bound to be social crusaders in some way or another.

Scorpio Rising

Scorpio is the only sign that's an octave away from itself. That means Scorpio rising people are exactly like Scorpios on the inside, regardless of what they're projecting on the outside. Just as with any other Scorpio, if you piss them off, they will bite your head off and not think twice about it. They'll be very uncomfortable if you try to hug them or touch them. Scorpios are very possessive and don't like to give things up. They get more possessive the older they get because people who have a rising sign in Scorpio tend to try to hang onto their youth more than any other sign of the zodiac.

Aloofness is a Scorpio characteristic. Scorpios are the best actors because they're so good at pretending, even to themselves. They don't like to show you what's really inside, and it takes a very long time for them to trust someone enough to reveal their inner core.

Capricorn Rising

If you have Capricorn rising, there are many things about you that people may find surprising. First, you're probably very good at seeming like someone who knows what they're doing. You know how to make big decisions quickly and really stick with them, but your decisiveness doesn't take away from your ability to listen to people and empathize with them. You may feel like you have a pretty good sense of what's right and wrong, even if you don't always adhere to those guidelines yourself. You can sometimes come across as being very serious, but you also have an amazing sense of humor that many people might not pick up on at first. You'll often focus on the more practical or intellectual things in life. It's important to you to feel like your lifestyle is sensible and stable rather than flashy, reckless, or indulgent. You've probably got a lot of friends, too.

Libra Rising

Libra is the sign that rules relationships, partnerships, beauty and ugliness, equality, social justice, and basically all things to do with diplomacy. So, if Libra Rising appears in your horoscope, you either have a talent for mediating disputes, know someone who does, or both.

Venus (the planet of love) rules libra. So, if you're Libra rising, you may be a people-pleaser. You might be beautiful or handsome and know how to use your appearance to get what you want, but it's also possible that the attention someone gives you is not enough and something inside of you feels unfulfilled.

Likely, you can't stand any form of injustice in your life or in the lives of others. You are probably a pretty good judge of character because, for Libra, it is easy to see people's motivations and hidden agendas behind their words or actions.

Chapter 4: Understanding the Birth Chart

Now let's talk about the birth chart, beginning with the houses of the horoscope. All the signs, planets, and houses make up your horoscope chart, which is basically a visual overview of what the sky looks like at any point in time. Think of it as a map of the entire universe, making it convenient for you to figure out where the position of each planet is in the sky. The various houses make splitting the chart into different sections easy.

The word horoscope comes from the Greek words hora, meaning "hour," and scopos, meaning "watching." It's the astronomer's job to read the natal chart just like a captain would take a look at their navigation system to make sure they're on track. Tarot readers and astrologers read the natal chart like a map of treasures and dangers so that you know where to go and what to absolutely avoid if you want to live your best life.

Space and Time

Charts are drawn up in the form of a circle because they represent the way we see the solar system from our little blue planet. The charts are split into 12 houses. Think of each house like a slice of pie, with each one representing each zodiac sign. Interestingly enough, the word "zodiac" means "circle of animals."

Astrologers need the houses of the chart to accurately find the planet's positions as they move through each sign. When you take a look at the birth chart, you can see the sign that a planet was passing through when you were born, and you can tell what the relationship between all the planets was to one another. These relationships are important as they make your life obvious. The houses bring another layer of astrological meaning to your life, but they also have extra useful information on their own.

Each month, the sun is placed in a different zodiac sign, but it moves through all twelve houses of the charts each day, along with the rest of the planets. This is because we not only revolve around the sun (which is why we move through the different zodiac signs each month), but the Earth also turns on its own axis, taking 24 hours to complete a full rotation. On account of all this spinning and twirling, each part of the Earth is exposed to a different zodiac sign for about two hours per sign.

This shouldn't confuse you. Just imagine the sun moving through the sky as it normally does each day, rising in one part and setting in another. On the chart, the sun, moon, and planets go through the different houses as the earth moves along through space. The houses show our point of view of the rest of the solar system as we continue to spin in our own place.

Houses are necessary and useful because they can offer us a framework to base astrological readings on. They give us background information and perspective concerning the planets as we continue to make our way through each sign. Each house has a meaning, which is rooted in the signs themselves.

The Natural Zodiac Map

The natural horoscope is a map of the sky showing each house of the chart being led by a zodiac sign. Since each sign is ruled by one of the planets, each house has its own planetary leader as well. For instance, Aries is in charge of the first house, which in turn is ruled by Mars. This means that Mars and Aries are connected to the first house of the chart.

When it comes to real-world applications, you'd be hard-pressed to find a natural horoscope chart that is perfect, with all planets neatly tucked into their designated signs and occupied by the correct owner, and that's because the planets are in constant orbit around the sun with their own rotations too. Add in the fact that the way we see the houses is in constant motion, and it's easy to realize that there's no way each planet will be in its designated house all the time since these calculations are made from the perspective of the Earth, which will never stop rotating. At the end, when a planet winds up in its own house and sign, it's usually accidental. Having said that, astrologers still have to be mindful of the natural horoscope when they're trying to read birth charts or other charts because the signs and planets in charge of a house will always wield some influence over them. Just because the signs and planets are hardly ever in their houses doesn't mean they don't own the homes outright.

Houses of the Zodiac

Let's take a look at the houses and what they rule and the signs and planets these houses are ruled by.

The First House: In charge of physical appearance as well as first impressions. Ruled by the ram Aries and connected to leadership. Its ruling planet is Mars, which is the planet of aggression and energy. The sign that is on this house's cusp is the ascendant or rising sign. You can think of this as the house where the sun rose when your life began. Out of all the houses in the zodiac, this one is known as the House of Self, and it can show people a lot about your personal views, self-image, drive, ambition, ego, appearance, and more. The planets you have in this house will definitely affect how you act and how others see you.

The first house is what determines everything you consider first in your life, which means it can affect your new beginnings, fresh starts, and the times you decide to take the initiative. It affects the new things in your life, the things that force you to think about what your potential is, who you really are, who you might eventually become, and what the best path to success is for you. The first house is critical to understanding your potential and how you can offer your light to the world. When you know more about your first house, you'll be able to understand your early experiences and why you wear the mask you do when you're interacting with people for the first time.

The Second House: This governs values, possessions, and money. Ruled by the bull Taurus and connected to the property, its ruling planet is Venus, which is the planet of attraction and love.

The second house, called the House of Possessions, asks you to consider what you value, what you own right now, and what you'd like to have in the future. It's about you are figuring out what motivates you to get the material things you want. There's more to this house than just the physical. It's about your emotions and feelings and your willingness to own and love yourself as you are. In other words, it's the house that's about your self-worth, security, and sense of self. It's the house that requires you to think about the connection between your emotions and your actions, especially when it comes to spending and making money. Does the way you make a living line up with your sense of self-worth, or is it out of alignment?

With this house, you have to focus on your five senses and the pleasures that come with them because it's ruled by the planet of pleasure and beauty, Venus. Think about how you feel about luxury. Do you long for luxurious things but aren't able to afford them? This house calls you to create a world that will make you feel satisfied with yourself.

The Third House: This house is responsible for neighborhoods, siblings, and communication. Ruled by the twins, Gemini, and connected to communication, its ruling planet is Mercury, which is the planet of communication and speed.

This is the House of Communication, which means it's about the way you relate with others, the way you think, your style of communication, language, connection with technology, and so on. It's the house that lets you know a mind is a powerful tool, very versatile, and worth harnessing so that you can share it with others and impact them powerfully.

This house is also about relationships with family, neighbors, and those who are a part of our tribe. It's also about libraries, early experiences in school, travel, community affairs, and teaching.

The Fourth House: This house is responsible for family, home, and motherhood. Ruled by the crab, Cancer, and connected to nurturing and protection, its ruling planet is the Moon, which is in charge of feminine cycles, the subconscious, and reflection. This house relates to all home matters. It's about what home means to you, and that isn't just about your literal home but your ancestral roots and where you will finally come to rest at the end of your days.

Since the home is where you feel safe, the fourth house is about being safe and feeling a sense of belonging. It's about real estate, traditions, customs, and family history. It's also about parenting, especially about the mother, or whichever parent or parental figure offers you the most security. It's the house of home and family.

The Fifth House: This house is in charge of recreation, procreation, and creation. It is ruled by the lion, Leo, who is connected to showmanship and courage. Its ruling planet is the sun, which is the source of enlightenment, light, and energy. This is the House of Pleasure, and its main focus is creativity and fulfillment. If something feels pleasurable and good, then it's connected to the fifth house.

This house is about romantic relationships and the pleasure you get from them. This house rules relationships, and it's about the satisfaction other people give you in terms of emotions or when there's any risk at play. For many people, it's exciting to live on the edge, taking risks financially, romantically, and so on. Even gambling is a part of this house. This is the house of hobbies, love, and games. It's the funhouse, literally, being connected to children and childishness. With this house, you can find the creative passion you had as a child and rediscover your hobbies.

The Sixth House: This house is in charge of others' services, responsibilities, duties, and work. It is ruled by the virgin Virgo, which is connected to health. Its ruling planet is Mercury, which is the planet of communication and speed. This is the House of Work and Health. It's about keeping your health in tiptop condition, which allows you to function at your best when it comes to working.

This house invites you to think about where you could do better to have a more balanced work-life relationship. You have to think about the areas of your life and see what bad habits you need to shed. The main themes of this house are personal growth, responsibility, and duty. You're called to think about your body, work out, eat right, and find some time to play while you work. This house also warns you against getting lost in trying to please others to the point where your own needs are disregarded. This house is about perfection, medication, diet, fitness, routines, and hygiene.

The Seventh House: This house is in charge of intimate relationships, partnerships, and marriage. Ruled by the scales, Libra is connected to balance, equality, and justice. Its ruling planet is Venus, which is the planet of attraction and love.

Also called the "House of Partnerships," it's the house that handles all partnerships in both business and personal lives, and it's about business deals, contracts, agreements, and more.

The house asks you to move your awareness from your own affairs and instead consider your life in terms of partnerships. When you choose to share, relate, cooperate, and interact with others, you'll gain wonderful treasures. When you connect with other people, you will achieve so much more than managing your affairs all by yourself. This is the home of sharing and commitment, and it's so much more than finding pleasure with other people. It's about creating bonds that last a lifetime and, for this reason, this house is in charge of matters like divorce, professional and personal enmity, lawsuits, separations, companionships, and platonic intimacy.

The Eighth House: This house is in charge of other people's money, death, and sex. Ruled by the scorpion, Scorpio, and connected with life's dark mysteries. Its ruling planet is Pluto, which is in charge of unavoidable change, resurrection, and death. The eighth house is the house of sex, too. It's about sharing resources, inheritance, physical, emotional, and financial support from others, and more. This is one of the more complex houses, as it encapsulates the mysteries of life, your secrets, and the unknown. The house is a deep one and has no room for the superficial.

A transformative house, you can find a passion for rituals, the occult, and more beneath this roof. The spiritual and the scary dwell together here. It's also about bad karma, crime, alimony, bankruptcy, insurance, taxes, control, and jealousy. This house is where the body and the soul become one.

The Ninth House: In charge of higher education, long-distance travel, and philosophy. Ruled by the archer, Sagittarius, which is connected to exploration and honesty, its ruling planet is Jupiter, the planet of expansion and luck.

The House of Higher Learning is about the higher mind, adventure, and opening up to new concepts. Spirituality and philosophy are at home here. It's about optimism and inspiration and bridging the divide between knowledge and skill. By traveling worldwide, you learn a lot by looking at other people's cultures and experiences. It's about a need to understand the world around you, other people, and yourself. The main focus areas of this house include ethics, psychology, spirituality, sociology, and philosophy. This house will lead you on your ultimate path and help you find a way to embody your ideals. It's about learning more about who you are through the eyes of strangers, looking at the mirror of the unfamiliar to find the pieces of yourself that make you. It's also about truth, collective thought, religion, journeys, publishing, international relations, writing, and books.

The Tenth House: This is in charge of authority figures, fathers, public image, career, status, and ambition. Ruled by the goat, Capricorn, which is connected to reward and work, its ruling planet is Saturn, which is in charge of limitations, boundaries, and structure. The House of Career is about who you appear to be in the public eye, your reputation, and your social status. The main themes of this house are prestige, success, fame, financial gain, and power. The house is in charge of how you fit into the world around you and the part you play, which involves much more than your career. It's about how much you embody your authentic self and your ego. The important questions to consider when dealing with the affairs of the third house are: How are you making use of your talents and gifts for good? Are you going to use them only to enrich yourself or to give back to others somehow?

The Eleventh House: In charge of long-term thinking, causes, and social groups, and ruled by the water bearer, Aquarius, which is connected with idealistic visions for a better life and world. Its ruling planet is Uranus, which is in charge of rebellion, revolution, and independence.

The House of Friends is the life of the party. It's a social house about gatherings, socializing, large groups, and community. It also covers humanitarianism, rebellion, and social justice. When it comes to matters of friendship, you must ask yourself if you're a good friend to your friends and what it is you do for them that makes you a good friend. What do you see in them, and what do they think of you?

This house also covers organizations, professional and personal clubs, and so on, specifically housing the idea that in numbers, you'll find strength. This house helps you discover the magic of teamwork, as two heads are better than one. Another thing is that when you're in organizations, whether they're professional, personal, or volunteer ones, you have the chance to grow in so many ways and gain more value in your life. This house is also in charge of your hopes, dreams, future, and long-term goals and achievements. It's about surprises, science fiction, inventions, trends, technology, collaboration, networking, and astrology itself.

The Twelfth House: In charge of hidden places, the occult, and psychic abilities. It is ruled by the fish, Pisces, which is connected to intuition. Its ruling planet is Neptune, which is associated with illusion and mysticism.

The House of Unconsciousness is definitely not about reality. It's about escapism, fantasy, dwelling on the positive rather than the negative. In this house are psychic abilities, dreams, and intuition. This is a very otherworldly space. This is the last zodiac sign, and therefore, it is connected to endings. It's also a house that is anything but superficial.

Also called the House of Reckoning, this house helps you go over your past actions so you can figure out what to do next based on the results you've achieved and whether you're satisfied with them. It's a private house that doesn't willingly or easily make known its weaknesses or strengths to the public, while the subconscious mind does its best to work through both. The house is in charge of the pain caused by bottling things up within you and chooses to pay attention to that which you've hidden and suppressed, sometimes even from your own self.

This final house is about seeing what your subconscious can teach you and how to use what you learn practically. Karma is important, which means you must deal with the consequences of your choices. This process could prove transformative for you. Don't assume the subconscious affairs ruled by this house only refer to the dark and murky stuff. They apply to the lighter imaginations and thoughts that you have, as well as the dreams that make your heart feel light. There is a flair for art and an undeniable creative streak here.

This house is also a representation of how you tend to get stuck in a rut or confined to routines in life and represents hospitals, prisons, and other such institutions. It's also about hidden agendas, alcohol, drugs, empathy, compassion, dance, music, art, sacrifice, old age, and life after death.

Angular Houses

The angular, or cardinal house is one of the horoscope's four cardinal houses. In these houses, you find the chart angles. The angular houses have the most power on your chart. They are in charge of the important things in life, such as family life, relationships, careers, and appearance. The first house is usually the ascendant, which can sometimes overpower the sun sign. The fourth house is usually the Imum Coeli, which represents your family, security, home, and endings in your life. The seventh house is usually the descendant, showing you the partnerships you will draw to yourself. The tenth house is the midheaven, which has to do with creative output, vocations, careers, and public persona.

Fixed Houses

These fixed houses are connected to Leo, Taurus, Aquarius, and Scorpio. They are the second, fifth, eighth, and eleventh houses. When your chart has a lot of these houses, this means you're likely fixed and not mutable. You find you're steadfast, can focus on the things that matter to you, and won't stop until you achieve what you want. You don't struggle with perseverance. You're resolute and determined, and you make a point of getting to the finish line on your tasks before going on to something else.

Mutable Houses

The third, sixth, ninth, and twelfth houses are mutable, and the signs they're connected to are Virgo, Gemini, Pisces, and Sagittarius. If you have a lot of these in your chart, that means you're mutable. You are flexible, and you know how to adapt to anything that comes your way. You'd rather conform if doing so means keeping the peace, and this ability to blend can help you go a long way in life.

You're very resourceful, know how to make the best of a bad situation, love to learn, and are the quintessential diplomat. You're sympathetic, smart, and have a sixth sense that is very active. The only thing is, when you want to please everyone, you get into trouble. So, learn to set boundaries.

How to Read a Birth Chart

To read your natal charts, you need to use the planets to guide you. Glyphs on the charts represent the planets, and you can also find alternatives to the glyphs on some charts. The placement of the planets represents different parts of your persona, so when people say your "Pluto is in Virgo," they mean that star sign is what influences the trait that is ruled by the planet.

The Sun glyph resembles a circle with a dot in the middle. The moon glyph is a crescent moon facing the left. Mercury's glyph looks like a circle with a cross beneath it and two protrusions on the left and right above the circle. Venus looks like Mercury's glyph, but without the protrusions. Mars is a circle with an arrow pointing upwards and to the right. Jupiter resembles the number four. Saturn resembles a small letter "t" with a letter "n" at the bottom, pointing at a 45-degree angle. Uranus looks like an H with a vertical line through the horizontal line of the H, resembling a cross. Neptune resembles a trident with a cross at the bottom, while Pluto also resembles a trident with a circle instead of a prong in the center. The symbol for rising is an arrow that points upwards.

What Each Planet Represents

Sun: The dominant personality and identity.

Moon: Emotions and the hidden, inner self.

Mercury: Technology, communication, travel, intelligence.

Venus: Beauty, love, how love and affection are given and received, attraction.

Mars: Assertion, aggressive, action, sex life, boldness.

Jupiter: Optimism, good fortune, truth, luck.

Saturn: Responsibility, challenges.

Uranus: Authenticity, originality, uniqueness.

Neptune: Creativity, artistry, dreams, imagination.

Pluto: Intensity, passion, obsession, self-involvement.

PART TWO: Meet the Cards

Chapter 5: Major Arcana and Astrology

The Fool

A young man is standing at a cliff's edge, carefree, and on a fresh, adventurous journey on this card. His eyes are looking up at the universe as though he's got no clue that he's about to step off a cliff and into the deep unknown. He has a knapsack on his shoulder with all he could ever need, and it's not much. In his left hand, he holds a white rose that stands for his innocence and purity, and at his feet, he has a little white dog that represents the fact that he's protected and has a loyal companion. Mountains surround the Fool, representing the obstacles and challenges he will face along the way.

Description

The Fool tells you that you should follow your fire. You're to do what your heart calls you to do, even if it feels scary, as your focus should be on the treasures and lessons you can learn along the way. The card encourages excitement and curiosity. If there's something you've been mulling over doing, the time to do it is right now. Have fun and relax.

When this card is reversed, it might mean that you're dealing with starting a new project, but you're not quite ready to get it up and running. It could also mean you're taking on too much risk, and you need to dial the recklessness back down a notch.

Correspondences

Element: Air

Planet: Uranus

Sign: Aquarius

Keywords

Upright: Spontaneity, new beginnings, innocence, adventure, faith, potential fearlessness, originality, a leap of faith, purity of action, freedom from constraints, being in the present, acting without malice, seeking freedom, eccentricity.

Reversed: Silliness, acting without thinking, stupidity, folly, chaos, not thinking through plans, poor judgment, no direction, gullibility, playing safe, naivety, restrictions, blocks, no adventure.

The Magician

Numbered 1, this card is the number that represents opportunities and new beginnings. The Magician has one arm stretched up toward the sky while the other points to the earth, representing the concept of "As Above, So Below." This is the idea that whatever you create in your mind, you will see in your life. It's the connection between the material and the spiritual that, when understood, can be used to manifest your desires. His white robe represents purity, and his red cloak represents worldly knowledge and experience. On the table are the tarot suits' four symbols; the cup, sword, pentacle, and wand, which represent water, air, earth, and fire. Above the magician's head is the infinity symbol. A snake bites its tail around his waist, acting as a belt. In the background, there are flowers and foliage.

THE MAGICIAN.

Description

This card is about using your resources to create your ideal life. You need to know that you already have everything you need, and you don't need to accumulate more. When reversed, it means you're looking into what you desire but not acting on it yet because you're unsure how to make it happen for yourself. You need to pay attention to what your intuition is telling you. It might be that you are no longer in touch with your why, so you need to find that again before you can find the inspiration and drive to make it happen.

Correspondences

Element: Air

Planet: Mercury

Signs: Virgo, Gemini

Keywords

Upright: Creative visualization, the direction of the will, willpower, gift of the gab, smooth-talking, self-employment, work, magic, technology, electronic, written, and oral communication, skill, manifestation, power, action, creativity.

Reversed: Feeling out of your depth, ill intentions, charlatan, fake skills, manipulation, the ill intention, stagnation in creativity, abuse of power, blocks in communication, liar, con artist, deception.

The High Priestess

The High Priestess is dressed in a blue robe and seated before a thin veil with pomegranate decorations. The veil is the barrier between the subconscious and the conscious, which is unseen and seen. On both sides of the priestess are two pillars that form the entrance to the mystic temple, which is connected to the Temple of Solomon. One of them is black, while the other is white. The black one has the letter B for Boaz, which means "in his strength." On the other white one is the letter J for Jachin, which means "he will establish." These pillars, being black and white, also represent duality. On her head is a horned crown, and on her chest is a cross. She holds a scroll with the word TORA on it, which is the greater law. At her feet is a crescent moon.

THE HIGH PRIESTESS

Description

In a reading, this card represents the fact that you have access to the underworld to gain the knowledge you need from deep within. It asks you to connect with your intuition using meditation, shamanic journeying, and finding your place in a spiritual group or with like-minded individuals. When reversed, it means you're not paying attention to critical information from within you. You need to slow down and remember that true change begins by going within to adjust what you must for the world to reflect back to you what you desire.

Correspondences

Element: Water

Planet: Moon

Sign: Cancer

Keywords

Upright: Sanctity, morality, a chaste woman, a single woman, finding your truth, spirit guides, higher self, things unrevealed yet, esoteric knowledge and wisdom, divination, emotional stability, spiritual insight, self-trust, inner knowing, intuition, and mystery.

Reversed: Blocked intuition, incorrect use of spiritual gifts, immorality, never listening, being deceived and lied to, secrets, withholding information.

The Empress

The Empress has blonde hair and has a calming, peaceful energy about her. She wears a crown decorated with 12 stars to demonstrate the connection between the natural cycles of the universe and the mystical world. Her robe has pomegranates all over it, representing the concept of fertility, and she's sat on a bunch of very luxurious cushions as well as red velvet. On a cushion is the symbol of Venus, which rules grace, beauty, fertility, creativity, and love, making up the essence of this card. The forest and stream around her show she's connected to Mother Earth and all of life. The water and trees bring her peace and rejuvenation. Wheat is a sign of abundance.

Description

This card is strongly linked to fertility, sensuality, elegance, nurturing, and creativity, all of which are in the realm of the feminine. Drawing this card asks you to connect with the divine feminine in you and find and build beauty in all aspects of your life. You may feel the need to be caring and nurturing, or you may be about to experience the birth of a child or an idea. It could also represent pregnancy, both literally and metaphorically. When reversed, you have to take care of yourself. You need to take all that nurturing energy and focus it on yourself.

Correspondences

Element: Earth

Planet: Venus

Sign: Libra

Keywords

Upright: Social status, successful opportunities for business, fulfilling potential, creative problem solving, pregnancy, multitasking, earth, businesswoman, beauty, love, mother,

mothering, fertility, abundance, nurturing.

Reversed: Laziness, depression, infertility, home problems, money problems, waste of resources, zero coordination, stagnation in business, stagnation in creativity.

The Emperor

Where the Empress is the mother, the Emperor is the father, seated on a large throne of stone decorated with the heads of four rams, representing this card's connection to Mars and Aries. He holds the Egyptian ankh in one hand, representing life, while the orb in his left is the world he reigns over. His red robe represents energy, passion, and power. His suit of armor beneath that shows protection from all threats and weaknesses. His flowing white beard is a sign of wisdom that comes with experience and age. His gold crown shows he's got authority that is recognized. The mountain range backing him shows he has a strong force backing him and won't make unnecessary changes. The small river tells us that regardless of how tough he seems, he does feel things, but you need to get him to trust you to see this side of his character.

Description

Drawing this card may mean you're taking on the role of a father, regardless of how you identify. You provide, protect, and defend. The card is the sign of a strong, respected leader with power and recognition. This is likely a role you're at ease with, ruling with strength and fairness. It's about expertise and knowledge, and you could be a boss, teacher, coach, or just someone who loves to share what they've learned with others. Reversed, this card asks you to look at how much control, power, discipline, authority, and responsibility you have. Is it too much, or not enough, and does that work in your favor? It could also mean you're not walking in your power at all and are letting others have it instead. Find ways to correct that.

Correspondences

Element: Fire

Planet: Mars

Sign: Aries

Keywords

Upright: Fairness, stability, responsibility, rational thought, firmness, taking a clear stand, law, order, ambition, self-assertion, promotion to a higher, more senior role, establishment, father, leadership, boss, authority, structure, order, authority.

Reversed: No promotion, lawlessness, no discipline, immaturity, power abuse, withdrawn support, laziness, cruel man, weak man, underachiever, control freak, autocrat.

The Hierophant

This card is the masculine form of the High Priestess. It's also called the Teacher or the Pope in some other decks and is ruled over by Taurus. The Hierophant sits between two pillars. These pillars mark the entrance to a temple. He has three robes on, one red, one blue, and one white. His crown has three tiers representing all the worlds he's in charge of: the superconscious, subconscious, and conscious. His right hand is raised in blessing with two fingers pointing towards heaven and the other two towards the earth, while his left hand holds the papal cross, representing his status in religion. Two followers are kneeling before him as they wait to receive spiritual wisdom from him. This represents the key concept of group identity and the need for a rite of passage to move on to the next level in life. At the hierophant's feet are a pair of crossed keys that represent the balance of the subconscious and conscious minds. This balance is necessary to reach the mysteries that only the Hierophant can teach.

THE HIEROPHANT

Description

This card is about set beliefs and values in terms of spirituality and is often connected with formal doctrines and religion. The Hierophant asks you to consider your basic principles before deciding your belief systems and choices. You may need assistance from a guide, mentor, or teacher to show you the beliefs and values in a structured manner. It could also represent your intention to serve as a teacher or mentor to others. When the court is reversed, you are called to remember that you're a teacher and that everything you need to know is within you. You need to stop following others blindly and find the truth within you. Don't get trapped or bogged down by dogma. Always question the status quo.

Correspondences

Element: Earth

Planet: Jupiter

Sign: Taurus

Keywords

Upright: Brotherhood, spiritual retreats, seeking advice and counsel, divine laws, mystical groups, occult groups, spiritual guidance, teacher, guru, religion, status quo, orthodoxy, tradition, learning, teaching, education, large institutions, group identity.

Reversed: Breakdown in crisis resolution, the rejection of religious ideas, withdrawal from or of education, the closing of social services, schools, and hospitals, extremism, abuse of power, abuse of position, false gurus, false gods, and cults.

The Lovers

On this card, you will see the angel, Raphael, standing over a naked woman and a naked man. Raphael's name translates to "God heals," which shows that emotional and physical wounds can be healed. The Angel's hands are outstretched over the man and woman in blessing. The lovers are standing in a lovely, beautiful landscape that resembles the Garden of Eden. Behind the woman is an apple tree. Around that tree, a snake winds its way up. The apple tree and serpent symbolize the temptation caused by our sensual desires and pleasures, making us forget about focusing on the divine. There is a tree of flames behind the man, symbolic of passion, which is his main concern. There are twelve flames in total, representing the 12 Zodiac signs and representing time and eternity. The man has his eyes on the woman, who has her eyes on the angel. This represents the path from the superconscious to the subconscious and the conscious, or from spiritual to emotional and physical. In the background is a phallic, volcanic mountain that shows the passionate eruption that occurs when the masculine and feminine within come together.

Description

This card is about meaningful relationships and connections. It is also about being completely honest and open with one another, as depicted by both lovers being naked and vulnerable. When it comes out reversed, it means that you are not in touch with those that you love. You find a lot of trouble in your relationships with them. It asks you to remember why you love them to begin with so that you can come back to being your loving self. On the flip side, it could also mean that it is time to move on from this lover or friend. It could also mean that your feelings for someone are not reciprocated. Reversed Lovers also tells you to respect and love yourself more.

Correspondences

Element: Air

Planet: Venus

Sign: Gemini

Keywords

Upright: Union, contracts, marriage, trust, harmony, choosing between one lover and another, engagements, commitments, falling in love, love affairs, duty-bound, entering business with others, togetherness, crossroads, affection, partnership, choices, love.

Reversed: Leaving someone, falling apart, failing business, failing, a deal gone bad, trouble in relationships, infidelity, fear of commitments, love affair broken, relationship over.

The Chariot

A warrior appears to be brave on this card, standing within a chariot. The crescent moons stand for desires coming into being. The square on his tunic represents the strength of his will. The alchemical symbols that he has on represent spiritual transformation. His star crown and laurel are signs of success, victory, and evolution in spirit. It may seem like he's driving the chariot, but you'll notice that he has no reins. This is because he moves it along using his mental power. The canopy of 6-pointed stars above his head represents his connection to the divine world. In front of his chariot are two sphinxes, one white and one black, representing divine duality. To further delineate the idea of duality, you will notice that the sphinxes pull in different directions. However, the charioteer can use his mind to get them to go where he wants them to go. Behind him, there was a wide river representing the idea of being in sync with nature's flow while pursuing your dreams.

THE CHARIOT.

Description

This card represents strength, determination, willpower, and making decisions that honor your values. Drawing this card is a sign of encouragement that you will achieve your goals as long as you remain disciplined and dedicated. Courageous action will serve you much more than passive hope.

When reversed, the chariot asks you to realize you're letting obstacles stop you from doing what you want and that things are getting harder. You need to get back to why you took up your goal to begin with. Also, make sure you're not biting off much more than you can chew.

Correspondences

Element: Water

Planet: Uranus

Sign: Cancer

Keywords

Upright: Energy, impetus, driving force, skill mastering, helping someone else, triumph over obstacles, success with no support, transportation, journey, success, victory, confidence, ambition, direction, willpower, drive.

Reversed: Needing someone's help, broken down vehicle, canceled trip or journey, losing ambition and drive, no will, going the long route, having no direction, scattered energy.

Strength

This is a woman stroking a lion's jaw and forehead, calming the symbol of desire and passion with her loving energy without using force. She works using her inner strength only. Her white robe represents purity, her crown and belt of flowers represent nature in bloom, and the infinity symbol above her head stands for infinite wisdom and potential.

Description

This card is like the Chariot in that it represents will, power, and determination, but the difference is that the strength here is an inner strength that helps you through life's obstacles. This strength is what gives you the confidence to deal with fears and obstacles, and it asks you to keep your animal instincts, unrefined emotions, and gut instinctive reactions in check.

Reversed, this card tells you that you might be out of balance, making you feel like you're lacking strength. You may have just had a setback that shook your confidence, but you're asked to remember your inner strength and that you have what you need to move forward. You might also be explosive in your behavior, so keep that in check.

Correspondences

Element: Fire

Planet: The sun

Sign: Leo

Keywords

Upright: Compassion, confidence with no arrogance, potency, virility, vitality, strength through nonviolence and personal power, heroic acts, eroticism, sexuality, sex, lust, enjoying power, confidence, patience, self-belief, self-control, self-assurance, inner strength.

Reversed: Hedonism, vanity, not sticking with personal moral code, overbearing, self-doubt, requiring support, not having courage, no patience, no self-control, fragility, weakness.

The Hermit

The Hermit is on a mountain top capped with snow, which stands for accomplishment, growth, and spiritual mastery. He holds a lantern in his right hand with the Seal of Solomon within it, representing the wisdom that lights his path, showing him only the next steps and not the entire path. He has a long staff in his left hand, representing the authority and power rooted in the subconscious mind, which offer balance and guidance.

Description

This card is about withdrawing from the usual routines of everyday life to go within and seek your answers. You need to separate yourself from the distractions on the outside to find your next course of action. It's time to be introspective and maybe even leave the materialistic world if you're so inclined so that you can focus more on your inner world.

When reversed, it means you haven't taken time to reflect on yourself, and you're taking on too much. You need to take time for spiritual practices like meditation. It could also mean you've isolated yourself far too much to the point where you're no longer connected to people.

Correspondences

Element: Earth

Planet: Mercury

Sign: Virgo

Keywords

Upright: Counseling, therapy, self-exploration, patience, withdrawing from society, home study, privacy, discretion, meditation, spiritual experiences, enlightenment, self-reflection, desiring solitude, contemplation, introspection.

Reversed: Sadness, being silenced, exile, loneliness, a social misfit, self-absorption, left out in the cold, isolation, turning your back on someone, withdrawing from those you love.

Wheel of Fortune

On this card is a giant wheel with a sphinx on top, Anubis (god of the dead) on the right, and the snake Typhon (god of evil) on the left. Typhon is also a life force entering the physical world. You'll see the letters TORA on the wheel, representing the Torah (law), rota (wheel), and tarot. In the middle wheel are alchemical symbols for salt, water, sulfur, and mercury, all life's building blocks. There are four winged creatures in each corner of the card, who are all angels connected to Aquarius, Scorpio, Leo, and Taurus. They're each holding the Torah.

Description

It's a reminder that life continues to go on just as the wheel will turn, and change is constant. So, if things are bad now, accept that they will change for the better soon. It's also a reminder that what goes around comes right back around, and you need to think about your choices for that reason.

When reversed, it means you should expect a turn in your fortune and luck, possibly for the worse. That doesn't mean you should sit back and let it happen, but that you should proactively mitigate your risks. Think about things you can do differently to weather the worst of the storm.

Correspondences

Element: Fire

Planet: Jupiter

Sign: Capricorn

Keywords

Upright: Success, good times, yes, winning games of chance, karma, chance meetings that are life-changing, destiny, fate, ups and downs, life cycles, movement, turning point, changes, opportunity, chance, luck.

Reversed: Bad times, no, unexpected and unforeseen setbacks, disappointments, difficult times, things not working out, failure, mishaps, misfortune, bad luck.

Justice

Justice sits on a throne before a purple veil representing compassion, between two pillars that stand for structure and law. Her right hand holds a sword representing logic, pointing up to represent finality in decisions, with a double blade that reminds us of the consequences of our actions. Her left hand holds the scales, showing that logic must be tempered with intuition to arrive at impartial decisions. Her crown has a small square representing orderly thoughts. She has a red robe on as well as a green mantle. Her little white shoe peeks out from beneath her robe.

Description

This card represents law, truth, fairness, and justice. You are held accountable for your choices, so it's smarter to line up with your Higher Self so you can act with integrity. If you need justice, that means you're going to get it soon, and when you do get a ruling, you're to simply accept it is what it is and move on.

When reversed, this might mean you've done something that goes against your morals, even if others don't know what it is yet. It's better to fess up and own your choices and then take action to correct yourself. It could also mean you're trying to pass the blame.

Correspondences

Element: Air

Planet: Venus

Sign: Libra

Keywords

Upright: Truth, justice, fairness, karma, legal affairs, dignity, integrity.

Reversed: Injustice, discrediting, legal flaws, inability to speak the truth, lies, unfair treatment, losing your case.

The Hanged Man

This card has a man with blond hair dressed in a blue shirt and red pants hanging upside down from a tree. He has his left leg bent at the knee and tucked beneath his extended right leg, and both hands are behind his back. The sun shines behind his head. His expression is peaceful, showing he's in this position of his own free will. His red pants represent passion, and his blue vest stands for knowledge.

Description

This card tells you there are times you must put off everything before taking your next action or let the divine handle it on your behalf in its own time. Let go of your fixed ideas about how and when things should happen. Let go of the old and trust your gut. Don't be in a hurry to act if your intuition says you should pause.

When reversed, it means you know you should pause, but you've refused to do that. Instead, you're overbooking yourself with too much work, projects, and more things that you have no idea who you are or what you want anymore. So set boundaries and refuse to take on too much. Don't jury into things. Clear your schedule and take some time off. The same can apply to relationships.

Correspondences

Element: Water

Planet: Neptune

Sign: Pisces

Keywords

Upright: Detachment from material affairs, spiritual advancement, experiencing change, letting go, giving up something, pause in activity, fresh perspective, new perspective, delay, crisis, breaking patterns, surrender, making sacrifices for gain, letting go.

Reversed: Attachment to the material, holding back, inability to let go, false motivations, holding on, coming back to life, resurrection, reemergence, not seeing all perspectives, not being open-minded, stuck in limbo.

Death

This card has a skeleton clad in black armor atop a black horse, carrying a black flag with a solitary white rose with five petals. This is death, its armor showing invincibility, its dark color representing mystery and mourning. The white horse represents purity, power, and strength. On the ground is a dead royal figure. A child, a woman, and a bishop beg death to spare them. In the background, a boat makes its way down a river, and on the horizon, the sun is setting between two towers.

Description

This card is often misunderstood, but there's no reason to be afraid when you draw it. It doesn't mean you'll die anytime soon. It represents the end of a major phase in your life, especially one that has outlived its purpose. Open yourself to the new. It's about change and transition, so you must let go of the old and be open to sudden change.

When reversed, it means it's time to let go, but you're being stubborn, or you don't know how to do that. You need to learn to surrender and trust that change always brings good things with it. Draw another card to have more insight into what it is you may have to get rid of.

Correspondences

Element: Water

Planet: Pluto

Sign: Scorpio

Keywords

Upright: Breaking old habits, rebirth, renewal, transformation, loss, failure, end of a cycle or era, cutting ties, releasing emotional attachments, dramatic change, mortality, endings in general.

Reversed: Repeating mistakes, not allowing change, going through the motions, unaware of life, inertia, depression, long-term terminal illness, not wanting to let go, holding on to the old and rotting, delaying endings.

Temperance

This card has an angel who is both feminine and masculine, with large wings, wearing a light blue robe with a square with a triangle on the front. The symbol represents the earthbound by nature's law. The angel has a foot on the rocks and another in the water, showing the importance of balance while going with the flow but remaining grounded. They pour water from one cup into another, showing life's alchemy. In the background is a path that winds its way up to a mountain range. A golden crown glows, hovering over the mountain.

Description

This card asks you to find balance and moderation in life. You need to stabilize yourself as you go with life's flow and choose to stay calm even in the midst of chaos and stress. Choose the middle ground so you can understand all perspectives. Be inclusive and choose moderation at all costs.

When reversed, this warns you that you've been very excessive, and you need to rein your actions in. Stop overdrinking, overeating, or overdoing anything. If you can't afford things, don't overspend. It also means there's something not quite right in your life, causing you tension. Pause and examine what that is and how you can remove it.

Correspondences

Element: Fire

Planet: Jupiter

Sign: Sagittarius

Keywords

Upright: Self-acceptance, starting self-therapy or self-help, seeking divine help, merging, connecting with guides, angel communication, combining opposites, choosing moderation, alchemy, synergy, blending, synthesis, balance, harmony.

Reversed: Ever giving and never receiving, feeling abandoned by your spirit guides, outbursts in anger, impatience, rising tempers, the start of illness, imbalance.

The Devil

The Baphomet is a prominent feature of this card. This half-goat, the half-man creature, is also called the Horned Goat of Mendes. He used to represent the balance that exists between the masculine and feminine and between good and evil. Sadly, this is a figure that has been scapegoated as purely demonic. He has a vampire bat's wings and stares hypnotically to entrance those who get too close, bringing them under his control. Above the Baphomet is an inverted pentagram, representing the darkness in the occult and magic. He has his right hand up in the air in the Vulcan salute and holds a flaming torch in his left. To his right and left are a woman and a man, respectively, with horns on their heads and chains around their necks that are connected to the pedestal on which the Devil is sitting. Both of them have tails, with a grape on the end of the woman's tail and a flame on the end of the man's, each representing pleasure and lust, respectively.

Description

This card is a depiction of your shadow self. It's a mirror that shows you the bad that you hold within yourself, the side of you that you keep hidden from everyone else. Drawing this card indicates that you may be trapped in a cycle of seeking short-term pleasure. You're under the grasp of negative thought patterns, relationships, behaviors, addictions, and more. You may assume that you have no control over those negative aspects of yourself, but that's not the case. Bring them to light and see how you can transmute them into something better.

When you get this card reversed, it means that you are right on the brink of leveling up or achieving something you've been working hard at for so long. However, to do that, you have to release all beliefs and limiting attachments that keep you from achieving your highest potential. You know exactly what it is. You need to let go of it. Cut it loose.

Correspondences

Element: Earth

Planet: Saturn

Sign: Capricorn

Keywords

Upright: Trapped with no options tethered to your job, working too hard, being obsessed, sexual gratification, sexual deviancy, unhealthy relationships, violence, lies, materialism, doubt, fear, addiction to money, drinks, drugs, and sex, enslavement temptation, bondage.

Reversed: Beginning a new life, freeing yourself from constraints, not allowing yourself to be overtaken by temptation, relationship with reduced sexuality, divorce, freedom from unhealthy addictions and relationships.

The Tower

This card has a tower on top of a rocky mountain, with lightning striking at it and lighting it up as two people escape from the windows, leaping head first with both arms outstretched. The tower stands solid but is built on dangerously shaky foundations so that only a single lightning strike brings it down. It's unclear where the two people will land when they hit bottom. There are 22 flames around them, standing for the 10 points of the Kabbalistic Tree of Life and the 12 Zodiac signs, telling you that even in the midst of chaos, the divine can intervene.

Description

We should expect the unexpected. This could mean chaos, destruction, or a really huge change. It could be anything from a personal disaster to a disaster that affects the entire world, and there's no way to escape it. The smart thing to do is to learn to accept what's going to happen and remember that it's a temporary thing and that you are never alone in these situations. Also, these somewhat cataclysmic and disastrous events tend to be for the highest good.

When this card is reversed, it means that you are going through a great personal change. This is a different kind of change. In the upright position, the changes are forced upon you while – in this reversed position – you are the one who is creating the change. You're asking yourself to take a deeper look into what you truly believe and if it serves you as intended. This can be a deeply uncomfortable period, but it's a good thing, and you have to trust that the outcome will be worth it for you. Pulling the reversed version of this court could also mean that you are delaying the inevitable destruction that is to come your way and that you are resisting the change, even though you know it's necessary. Relax and accept that it is what it is and that good things will come of it in the end.

Correspondences

Element: Fire

Planet: Mars

Sign: Virgo

Keywords

Upright: Home repossession, being ousted, being overthrown, losing your job, redundancy at work, bankruptcy, damage or an accident in your home, renovation, breaking down the old, revelation, release, catastrophe, destruction, upheaval, ruin, unexpected and sudden change.

Reversed: Still feeling the effects of resolved problems, cleared blockages, calm after the storm, illness, being afraid of the worst, volatile situations, disruptive people, milder losses, difficulties, obstacles, disruptions, continued and prolonged upheaval.

The Star

This depicts a naked woman. She kneels at the edge of a small pool with two containers, one in each hand. The left represents the subconscious, and the right the conscious. She pours water on the earth to encourage fertility, and the water runs into five rivulets that stand for the five senses. She empties the water from the other container into the pool. She has one foot on the ground and the other in the pool, representing practicality and intuition, respectively. Her nakedness is purity and vulnerability. A solitary large star shines in the night sky, standing for her essence, and the smaller ones are seven in number, representing the chakras.

Description

This card represents a reprieve after a chaotic time. It's what's left after you've rid yourself of limiting beliefs. You now know who you really are, and you know that no matter how bad things are, you are in touch with the Divine, and it protects you and will never leave you on your own. This also represents your quest for meaning and purpose in life, as you've now stripped yourself of all nonessentials and are ready to embark on the next great adventure.

Reversed means you no longer trust the universe because the challenges that have come your way feel like too much of a burden to bear. You don't know why you're being thrown a curveball after curveball, and each one seems to come at you larger, faster, and harder. It's hard to see that the Divine still supports you, but when you really look closely, you'll realize you're not alone, and the curveballs are lessons you need to learn. As soon as you look for the lessons and learn them, you can move past this phase.

Correspondences

Element: Air

Planet: Uranus

Sign: Aquarius

Keywords

Upright: Alternative therapy, peaceful period, inspiring person, healing, good health, making a wish, the heavens, astronomy, astrology, aesthetics, beauty, all forms of help, divine blessings, spirituality, renewal, optimism, opportunities, happiness, hope.

Reversed: Obstacles to spiritual enlightenment, obstacles to renewal, refusing to help, refusing to be helped, missing opportunities, disappointments, not feeling well, hopelessness.

The Moon

This card has the full moon at night between two prominent towers. The moon represents the unconscious, dreams, and intuition. The moonlight illuminates the winding path to higher consciousness that lies between both towers. A small pool in the foreground represents the subconscious mind, and a little crayfish crawls out of it, representing the unfolding of consciousness in the beginning. A wolf and a dog are on a grassy field, both representing the wild and tamed parts of the psyche, howling at the moon.

THE MOON..

Description

This card is a picture of your illusions and worries, and it's about the fact that you're being fearful about your present and future on account of what you've experienced in the past. It feels perfectly logical to be plagued by worry, but beware that they don't keep you from taking another stab at things. This is a period of uncertainty, and you need to be wise about making decisions. Don't rush, but instead, check in with your intuition before you act. Watch yourself talk for negativity and look into your dreams to see what they're trying to tell you.

Reversed, this tells you the negative thoughts, worries, and anxieties that once gripped you are dying down, especially as you've continued to work through them and realized how badly they'd affected you. It could mean you're burying these feelings, and while this may work for a short time, the more lasting solution is to address them right away. It could mean you're getting intuitive messages but aren't clear on what they imply. Slow down and really pay attention. Keep a dream journal and look for parallels between your dreams and waking life.

Correspondences

Element: Water

Planet: Neptune

Sign: Pisces

Keywords

Upright: Increase in psychic experiences and abilities, secrets, deception, no clarity, difficult times, dark night of the soul, mental confusion, visions, falsehood, mystery insecurity, hidden enemies, hidden things, illusion, nightmares, dreams.

Reversed: Irrational behavior, irrational thoughts, unusual sleeping patterns, insomnia, psychic insights that are unclear, unusual dreams, unveiled mysteries, revealed deceptions, the hidden becoming known, secrets being revealed.

The Sun

There's a large sun that shines brightly in the sky, giving life to one and all. Four sunflowers stand tall, bathing in the sunlight above a brick wall. These are the Minor Arcana's four suits and the four classical elements. A young child sits naked on a calm white horse in the foreground. This is the joy of being connected with the inner spirit, having nothing to hide, being innocent and pure as a child.

THE SUN .

Description

This card is about abundance and success, as the sun fuels you with strength in all you do. Your positivity serves you and brings you even more to be joyful about. You draw people to you because of the light you're radiating. If you're going through a tough time, the sun tells you things are about to change for the better. It also tells you to expect more goodness and energy. Channel that energy into something productive.

When reversed, this card asks you to let your inner child out already and find yourself. You've probably spent too much time being stuck in the drudgery of work and life that you no longer know what play means. It could also mean you're having a hard time being optimistic about your goals, feeling depressed, and no longer finding joy in work. The great thing about this card is that it's not a terrible thing even when it is reversed. What you're going through is temporary and can stop when you determine it's time to end it and create your own joy.

Correspondences

Element: Fire

Planet: Sun

Sign: Leo

Keywords

Upright: Conscious mind, masculinity, male archetype, good weather, nice holiday, good fortune, blessings, optimism, success, good times, clear thinking, marriage, riches, the energy of yes, happiness, manifestation, warmth, enlightenment, joy, vitality, energy, life.

Reversed: False ideas, false impressions, things not being as great as they appear, extra sentimental, delayed happiness, delayed success, less vitality, being under the weather, hope for better days, sadness, partial success.

The Judgment

This card has naked women, men, and children coming out of their graves with outstretched arms. Every eye looks up to the sky, where Archangel Gabriel blows the final trumpet, and all respond to this call to receive their judgment and see if they make it through the pearly gates or not. An impressive mountain range stands in the background, representing the futility of avoiding being judged as well as obstacles that are impossible to overcome.

Description

This card asks you to connect with higher consciousness to attain your grandest ideals for your highest good. It's the card of spiritual awakening as you come to realize there's so much more to your life than you've always thought. This represents attaining even greater heights on a cosmic level. You need to release your old self and become who you were meant to be. You're at an important point along your journey, and it's time to leave the past behind you and purge yourself.

When reversed, you must evaluate yourself using contemplation and meditation, as there are things you've hidden and tucked away, parts of yourself you've denied because of your worry about how others will perceive you or judge you. You need to forgive yourself for past mistakes, let go, and grow into your new self. The universe is calling you to be more, but you don't want to heed the call because you'd rather play it safe. It won't stop calling you, though, so the sooner you answer and trust that things will work out, the better.

Correspondences

Element: Fire

Planet: Pluto

Sign: Libra

Keywords

Upright: Moving on, judgment, final outcomes, making decisions, transition period, a rite of passage, end of an era, change that's already happened, realization, reincarnation, a religious or spiritual calling, call to action, renewal, awakening, rebirth, redemption.

Reversed: Unhealed karma, avoiding decision making, impending but delayed change, allowing fear to lead, self-doubt, awareness that your actions are bad for you, ignoring your calling.

The World

A naked woman with a purple cloth wrapped around her in a spiral; she dances in the center of a laurel wreath, looking back toward the past while her body urges her on to the future. In both hands, she holds wands like the magician's, signifying the completion of the manifestation process. A lion, cherub, bull, and eagle surround the wreath, representing Leo, Aquarius, Taurus, and Scorpio, the four cardinal points, seasons, and elements. They offer guidance as you move from one phase of life to another.

Description

This means you feel complete, fulfilled, and whole. You've finally wrapped up a project or relationship. It's the end of your purpose as it comes to pass, bringing you to where you've always wanted to be. Now it's time to reflect on how you got there. Take some time to bask in your glory and how you were able to overcome obstacles. It's time to show some gratitude for what you've gained rather than plunge headfirst into something new and big.

When reversed, it means you need closure on something. You might still feel emotionally attached to a relationship from the past and have to move on, or you might need to let go of impossible and unrealistic goals so you can focus on better things right now. It might mean there's a huge project you're supposed to finish, but you can't bring yourself to do that. Remember why you started and what it would mean to you to finally get it done.

Correspondences

Element: Fire

Planet: Saturn

Sign: Capricorn

Keywords

Upright: Studying cultures, socializing, anthropology, exploration, world travel, achievement of a goal, journey's end, successful conclusion, success, moving abroad, totality, success, wholeness, realizations, outcomes, possibilities, fulfillment, completion.

Reversed: Stuck in a rut, noncompletion, incomplete work, stagnation, non-movement, delayed success, unfinished business, interrupted house move, plans to fail.

Chapter 6: The Court Cards and Astrology

There are 16 court cards in a tarot deck. Each suit has a King, Queen, Knight, and Page. These are the cards that represent the individuals in our lives that influence situations in our lives, like our friends, family, and colleagues. The cards also tell you about the energy you're putting out or the energy you need during the reading. There are so many interpretations possible, which is why they can be confusing, so it's best to interpret them based on the context of the question you began the reading with.

Another worthwhile thing to note is that just because these cards are based on gendered roles, like the Queen being feminine while the King is masculine, you need to know that you don't have to think in gendered terms. For instance, you could be in "king mode" if you're at work and in "queen mode" when taking care of your pets, kids, or plants. It doesn't matter how you identify yourself. The kings are about authority and control, the queens are about caregiving and support, and knights are about action, while pages are about incoming messages, realizations, and news, as well as young people and kids in your life. The suits affect the daily changes and emotions that are subtle. Here's what each suit represents:

- **Cups:** relationships.
- **Pentacles:** financial matters and practical affairs
- **Swords:** Truth and conflict
- **Wands:** Creativity

Each card is connected to astrological elements, as you'll soon discover. With all this background information for context, let's begin by looking at the cups.

The King of Cups

This is connected to Scorpio. This king is in charge of an underwater world, choosing to go deeper and deeper into life's mysteries. Elementally speaking, all four kings in the tarot are intellectuals of the air. The King of Cups embodies air's intellect and water's emotion. This is the father and husband, a fixed water sign, which means he's a ruler full of passion and intensity, very analytical and perceptive. He is as sensual as he is smart, seeking to connect with someone on equal intellectual footing. He is at home with deep emotions and can be rather obsessive. His major arcana card is Death, with Pluto being the ruler of that card and the underworld's god. This king is in tune with time's ebb and flow, moving along with the natural rhythms of birth and change. He resembles King Neptune in the Wizard's tarot, wearing a crown with three prongs and bearing a trident that signifies his authority, while his white hair and beard represent experience and wisdom. This king makes nature do his bidding and is in charge of Libra's third decan as well as Scorpio's second decan. In the horoscope, he rules the eighth house, which is the realm of death, sex, joint resources, and inheritance.

The Queen of Cups

This queen is connected to cancer. She is about maternal devotion and emotions. An emotionally deep character, she has twice the traits of water. She is often drawn in the context of relationships and love, which are both watery worlds. Being cancer, she's clearly a natural caregiver and homemaker. Her love, sensitivity, care, and nurturing are unrivaled. She is the quintessential mother, who makes her a powerful force. A cardinal sign, she is decisive in her leadership. She's the reason we say, "The hand that rocks the cradle rules the world." The Charioteer is her counterpart, and she moves through dangerous, powerful tides and currents while staying away from rocky cliffs. She finds balance in family and marriage life. Naturally artistic and creative, her intuition knows no bounds. She tends to get mystical visions and make psychic prophecies on account of being ruled by the moon. She has a dark side to her, and the strength of her emotions can be dangerous. She could sometimes be a tad smothering and overprotective. She's in charge of Cancer's first and second decans, as well as Gemini's third decan. She rules over the fourth house, which is the domain of family and home life.

The Knight of Cups

This is a watery and emotional knight, equally generous, graceful, and gallant. He's a visionary with an extraordinary imagination, an idealist who sees the truth in beauty and vice versa. The Knights are the members of the court who go on rescue missions and adventures, so they have a lot of fire in them. They combine fire with their suit's element, and therefore, the Knight of Cups is both fire and water. He represents Pisces, a mutable water sign, sensitive, sweet, beguiling, and quite the charmer. However, he can be forgetful, fickle, and a little immature. The Moon is his counterpart, veiling his world with a mist as he dwells on the hopes, dreams, and wishes of the people around him. This knight is a romantic artist unafraid of emotions, in touch with his intuition, quite a catch, and yet ever elusive. He's in charge of Aquarius's third decan and Pisces' first and second decans. He rules the twelfth house, the domain of hidden secrets and mysticism.

The Page of Cups

She is water personified; graceful, unpredictable, still, choppy, effervescent, or smooth. She is the unification of Cancer, Pisces, and Scorpio, all watery signs. Like water, she can adapt, taking on the roles she must take depending on the situation. She tends to match the emotions that she can detect around her. Her preferred method of communication is through psychic impressions and dreams. Sometimes, her messages are subtle, and other times they can be a little too hard to miss. She has youthful exuberance around her and is often very willing to learn. She's kind and gentle, imaginative, and dreamy, an artist, a poet, and very optimistic. She has the Ace of Cups, which belongs to Juno, who's the goddess of childbirth and marriage. She drinks from this cup and receives the wisdom that comes from experience.

The King of Pentacles

This is an experienced man who has the keys to the kingdom, is successful, and who rules his entire world. This king mixes the elements of air and earth and represents Taurus, a fixed zodiac sign. Taurus's Taurus makes him steady, stable, and reliable. He is grounded, practical, dependable, and realistic in all his affairs. Hard work is his anthem. While some may think of him as being slow to act and stubborn, he is a persevering and patient king. His counterpart is the Hierophant, and so he loves tradition. Everything around him is a reflection of his spiritual values. He rules all kingdom affairs with a precision that can only be termed "mathematical." He's great at finding practical solutions that are out of the box for really complicated issues. Slow to anger, he's not to be trifled with when his patience finally runs thin, as his fierceness is intimidating. He's not particularly refined and is too earthy to be bothered with frivolities, but you will find him a loyal friend. His entire being is dedicated to whatever he sets his mind to. He is in charge of Taurus's first and second decans and Aries' third decan. He rules the second house, the home of personal belongings and values.

The Queen of Pentacles

This queen encompasses water and earth, fertility, and resourcefulness. She's intractable and patient. Connected to Capricorn, a cardinal earth sign, she's excellent when it comes to business and can create resources seemingly out of nothing for her subjects. An intractable woman, she is rooted strongly in her values, and from these values, she can bloom. She's an excellent decision-maker and leader, authoritative and down-to-earth. She is not quick to make rash decisions, exercises caution and discipline, and is not the sort who quickly does away with tradition. She's enduring and patient, which is why she takes her time to process things mentally. Her dry sense of humor often catches us off guard, and she's an old soul who has the youthful aura of a child. This queen guards the Earth because she understands it's not just for her or those around her but also for those yet to come. She has no time for theories that hold no water or are so stingy with resources because she understands that the Earth is more abundant than many people realize and will be here long after we're all gone. Her counterpart is the Devil, and she's aware of the pleasures that the flesh can offer, as well as the enchanting temptations that the earth possesses. She rules Capricorn's first and second decans, Sagittarius' third decan, and the house of social status and career, which is the tenth house.

The Knight of Pentacles

This is no ordinary knight, as he doesn't fit the usual description of what a knight should be. He's not the flirty sort, and he moves slowly. Other knights seek adventure, but he chooses to remain at home so that he can take care of the kingdom itself. This knight is the embodiment of fire and earth. As you know, the earth cannot burn, and dirt can put out small fires. He's of the earth, and the earth is fixed, never moving on its own. It takes natural phenomena like avalanches, landslides, and earthquakes to make this grounded knight move. He is the one who is most aware of physical needs, more so than the others. He desires mastery over the material world. When he has a mission in his mind, he will see it through to the end, no matter what it takes. This knight is very calm and has had patience for days. He is analytical, discerning, and particular about looking over details that others miss or don't deem important. He represents mutable Virgo, and his counterpart in the major arcana is the hermit. He is a conscientious knight, cautious, conservative, and quite a perfectionist. This knight rules Virgo's first and second decans and Leo's third decan. He's also primarily in the sixth house, which involves work, health, and service to others.

The Page of Pentacles

She has the energy of all earth signs – Virgo, Taurus, and Capricorn – and with this groundedness, she connects the Pentacles suit to all things relating to the physical world. She is young, but she has the nature of the earth, being down to earth herself. She's stable, dependable, and secure. She aspires to have a solid foundation to comprehend the physical realm. Her gait may be slow, but it is forceful and sure. She has great skill and is careful in all she does, which is why she's not keen on taking unnecessary risks. She is conscientious and consistent, very deliberate, and diligent. She has nurturing qualities like Mother Nature herself, and while she may be yet to be untilled ground, she will eventually act as a vessel for the birthing of the physical. Her duty is the protection of the physical realm.

The King of Swords

Connected to Aquarius, this airy intellectual has authority and power. All his decisions are based on solid intellect and logic. He is fire and air. Alert and assertive, this king is aggressive when needed, guarding his own with force and undeniable passion. He's not a stranger to arbitrary decisions and can mete out justice while defending his position in line with his rule. This king is idealistic, determined, and a forward-thinking person. He could be your best friend or your worst enemy. Socially conscientious, his counterpart is the Star, and from his vantage point, he has no problem seeing the big picture. Just like Uranus, he can upend old ways of doing things to create new and better institutions for the good of all. He is in charge of Gemini's first and second decans, Taurus's third decan, and the house of communication, which is the third house.

The Queen of Swords

QUEEN of SWORDS.

The Queen of Swords is connected to Libra. She is the combination of air and water, using her intellect and emotions to rule with both head and heart, therefore arriving at fair decisions. She blends logic with feelings beautifully. She thinks critically, is clever in conversations, and possesses a keen wit, intelligence, and sometimes a biting tongue. She is aware of the precision and power of words and their meanings, and she is the master of subtext. She knows how to whittle through useless information to get to the heart of the matter, regardless of the topic. She is aware that as powerful as words are, they don't do well when it comes to expressing deep-rooted emotions, so she can hear what isn't being said in all disputes and debates. She's compassionate and clear-headed, a firm ruler who is fair in her decisions. She has had much experience with heartbreak and sorrow and is often thought of as a divorcee or widow who has found the treasure in loss and knows how to empathize with others thanks to her own familiarity with pain. She is able and willing to factor in all sides of all stories, being the judge, mediator, and peacemaker all at once. The Justice card is her counterpart, and she judges based on the facts. Like Venus, who rules Libra, she is very drawn toward others. She is in charge of Libra's first and second decans and Virgo's third decan. She rules the house of relationships and partners, the seventh house.

The Knight of Swords

This knight combines fire with air and can ride as swiftly as the wind. He matches the perfect picture of a knight, being a brave warrior with enviable skill. He is always put together, has well-polished armor, and his horse is ready to go. However, there are times when he can be indecisive and sometimes even deceitful. However, he's the most chivalrous person you'll ever meet. He's the quintessential knight, ready to duke it out in a battle of concepts and ideas, fearlessly, energetically, and with enthusiasm. He loves to explore all ideas and traverse the furthest reaches of his imagination. A fearless adventurer, he is unaware of the concept of the ground beneath him, and gravitation cannot hold him. He represents Gemini, the mutable air sign, which is why he is a quick thinker and quite versatile. His aspirations are rather lofty, and he has his head in the clouds. He is never in one place longer than necessary, and you'll often find him jetting off on some new adventure. He is connected to the Lovers card of the major arcana and is interested in all sorts of experiences and people. He loves to communicate and share ideas and also uses some wit and panache. He rules the first and second decans of Gemini and Taurus' third decan. He is mostly in the house of communication, which is the third house.

The Page of Swords

This page combines all air signs – Aquarius, Libra, and Gemini. She moves fast and is very at home regarding advanced communication and intellect. She is inquisitive and intelligent, and with her clear head, she can see far ahead. She's alert, so nothing gets past her, and she is incredibly versatile, moving from one topic to another with ease and skill. She is at home with communication, and her thoughts and voice profoundly affect others. She could be gentle or forceful, but either way, you will feel her power when she speaks – and when she is silent. She may remain invisible or choose to hold her peace, but you will find it hard to deny her presence. She is youthful, possessing a child's enthusiasm and a thirst for learning and knowledge. She is all about possibility, and she is likely to have lots of students, ideas, and teachers in her wake. She is like the goddess of wisdom, Pallas Athene, full of reason and logic, both of which she uses to ensure justice and truth prevail.

The King of Wands

This king is connected to Leo, possessing the sign's fiery passion and spirit. He is a mix of air and fire, a monarch radiating courage and confidence connected to the major arcana card of strength. Brave and forceful as the sun, he inspires and lights up the world of those around him. He is at home, being the center of attention and paying attention as well. In this way, he is the most charismatic of the kings, having lots of admirers who are inspired by his rule because he offers them the ability to voice their deepest desires, and in the process, he fuels them with his own self-awareness and pride. This means he can be dramatic, egocentric, egotistical, and quite a dictator sometimes. He can be aggressive, acting with force and exploding at a moment's notice. He isn't afraid to declare scorched earth when he wants to make his stand clear. He embodies fire's purifying and cleansing power, and he demonstrates the renewal that comes after everything burns. As fierce as he can be, he is also playful. He is in charge of Leo's first and second decans and Cancer's third decan. He also finds a home in the fifth house, the home of procreation and recreation.

The Queen of Wands

This queen is a combination of fire and water, full of passion, energy, fire, and heat. She is a seductress – powerful and with simmering passion. She is a very mature woman who exudes grace in all she does and with no effort. She is mesmerizing, willful, sinewy, strong, dynamic, self-assured, and confident. She is spontaneous, and attempting to contain her is a laughable and futile exercise. She can be impetuous, impatient, and impulsive. She is brazen, bold, brave, and a warrior at heart. She is connected to the Emperor of the Major Arcana. A direct woman, she moves with speed, and her energy feels masculine as she chooses to be aggressive and direct, unafraid to assert herself suddenly and with force. She is in charge of Aries' first and second decans and Pisces' third decan. She is also at home in the first house, which is the house of self-expression and self-identity.

The Knight of Wands

This knight knows how to hold you spellbound. When he has no room to burn, this makes him get out of control, and he can be rather destructive, violent, and unstable. This is the one court card that combines fire with fire. An explorer, he has a very wide variety of interests and is interested in spiritual and philosophical conquest. He loves foreign ideas and people and will do all he can to traverse the world because he believes there is much to see and experience. He wants to meet everyone and taste all the experiences life offers him. He is connected to the Temperance card, and he loves to experiment, combine things, and adapt as needed. A restless knight, he's very impulsive and loves to be on the move. He represents

Sagittarius' fire, making him rather audacious and outgoing. He's the most carefree knight, and he believes in trying everything once – or more than once if he decides he loves the experience or wants more of it. He has the good fortune of Sagittarius, and so he considers himself invincible, which could lead him to act recklessly and engage in dangerous, risky activities. He's also one of the first to let you know he's fine with going out with a bang. He rules Sagittarius's first and second decans and Scorpio's third decan. He finds a home in the ninth house, which is the home of higher education, philosophy, and long-distance travel.

The Page of Wands

This is fire personified, the representation of all three fire signs: Sagittarius, Aries, and Leo. She is very enthusiastic when it comes to spiritual understanding and development. This page is pure and holy, and she acts as a vessel to allow spiritual creation. She is similar to Vesta, who is the goddess of home and hearth, and she is representative of the many generations of women who are in touch with their spiritual side and can trace their spiritual origins to her. She connects the Wands suits to creativity and spirit, and she is the one who keeps the flame of the Ace of Wands. She is youthful with childish exuberance, just like the other pages, and she loves to learn. She can lay low for a long time, but as soon as you pique her interest and feed her imagination, she flares up with interest and passion. It's hard to contain her excitement at this point.

Chapter 7: The Cups and the Water Signs

The Cups are considered one of the non-elemental "water" signs, connected to Scorpio, Pisces, and Cancer. The Cups suit is also called the suit of Goblets of Chalices. They are also considered feminine, feeling, an emotional sign that is intuitive in nature. This makes for an interesting water sign ruler regarding the typical personality associated with these astrological signs. Three key personality traits seem to be typical of this water sign:

- *They're empathetic and sensitive to the emotions of others.* These individuals tend to get caught up in the drama of life, and they may feel personally responsible for how others around them feel. If someone is upset, these people will take it on as their own responsibility and try to fix things. They truly care about other people, and this emotional empathy can make them very sensitive and highly supportive of those around them. Because they are so empathetic, it is easy for others to take advantage of these people and their goodwill.

- *They're imaginative, creative, and perhaps a bit impractical when it comes to real-world concerns.* This is the sign that is associated with daydreaming and flights of fancy. They have a knack for creative imagination that many people do not possess. Some might consider them "flighty" or impractical, but they would probably just disagree. These individuals also tend to have an artistic nature, which allows them to express themselves in unique ways when it comes time for play.

- *They're intuitive and perceptive.* What some might consider being psychic ability, these individuals are very good at looking below the surface of life. They are natural psychologists in many ways because they know how to read people rather easily. This insight allows them to pick up on small details that would often go unnoticed by most other people. They are also very good at anticipating what is ahead, and they tend to be on the right path in life.

Keywords

Upright: Beauty, aesthetics, empathy, serenity, calm, fluidity, flexibility, expression, culture, domesticity, the unconscious, nurturing, tactile, compassion, spiritual, artistic, romantic, dreams, love, sensitivity, romantic, relationships, caring, imaginative, receptive, passive, psychic, affectionate, clairsentient, intuitive, creative.

Reversed: Selfish, tearful, too sentimental, emotional, pessimism, negativity, loss, illogical, unresponsive, moody, unfeeling, cold, uncaring, fantastical, neglectful, intense, codependent, needy.

The Ace of Cups

An ace in playing cards is a symbol of hope or a new beginning. The Ace of Cups in the Rider Waite Tarot deck represents feelings and emotions. On this card, you see two cups with water overflowing, representing strong emotions that are hard to control. These emotions come out when these people act on their impulses or act when they feel, not when they think.

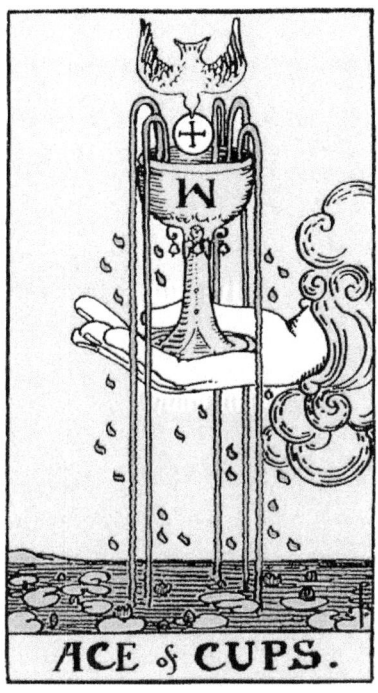

These people are naturally sensitive and emotional. They value feelings over all other things in life, including logic and common sense. Their emotions, especially love and hatred, are very powerful tools that can make or break them. Their greatest strength is their heart, while their greatest weakness is their ability to be swayed by appeals to their feelings.

These people care about others and love unconditionally. They place great value on emotional bonds, especially friendship and love, and they form strong emotional bonds quickly. Family ties are also quite important to them. They care deeply for their family members and will do anything for them. They can even let their emotions get in the way.

The Ace of Cups in reverse denotes feelings that are not expressed, resulting in negative consequences. The person cannot control their strong emotions and fails to see the warning signs around them. They may also be overwhelmed by their feelings and have trouble keeping up with them.

This card can represent an unrequited love or unfulfilled desire. They may have a hard time expressing how they feel and letting people know what they want. The person may also be going around in circles, being pulled between different feelings.

The Ace of Cups reversed can also indicate that the seeker will soon be overwhelmed by strong emotions or their own desires. In any case, it is a warning to the seeker to be more in control of their feelings.

Two of Cups

The Two of Cups, like the Two of Wands, is a card about duality. This time it's not just one person looking at themselves in a pool, but two people: a man and a woman sharing something together. They're standing in the same pose, and they both have cups on their chests that are touching. The meaning is very similar to the Two of Wands: partnership. There may be some element of romance here, but not necessarily – after all, this could be two friends sharing an understanding as easily as lovers meeting for tea. Making any relationship work requires focus and commitment. If you devote yourself entirely to another person or another venture, you open yourself up to great rewards but also great losses. Sometimes you have to risk everything for a dream, but sometimes dreams are just illusions. If you need help making a big decision, this card could encourage you to work with someone.

Three of Cups

The Three of Cups can mean celebration. This time, the cups from Ace and Two have been joined by two more. There's even a third hand reaching out from behind one cup as if it's about to grab another one. The three figures appear younger and happier than before, and there is a child among them now. They're dancing around a central point while holding their cups in the air triumphantly – all except one figure, looking away from the others toward something else, still holding her cup up high. There's definitely a feeling of celebration and triumph here. The Three of Cups is one of the most positive cards in the deck; it represents harmony and unity. You may be looking forward to some great achievement or success – maybe you're finally graduating from college after years of hard work, or your new business deal has come through at last, or perhaps you simply deserve to take some time out for yourself and spend an evening with friends dancing around like idiots while you drink yourself stupid (note: this card can also mean that).

Four of Cups

The Four of Cups shows us another related symbol: four cups are now placed around a central point instead of three, but they are all facing downwards towards the earth. A male figure passes by them with his head bowed, shuffling along with only one foot turned towards the cups. He's not really looking at them or even acknowledging that they're there at all. It's almost as if he doesn't notice them. All four figures are dressed in lighter colors, which makes sense because all of their cups are empty rather than having anything inside. Their skin is dark, and they have a small blue dot on their foreheads (similar to Shiva or Krishna). It seems like whatever kept them "grounded" previously has been lost, so they've gone back to being more spiritual figures who have walked away from worldly matters just as before. With no drink available to him, the first figure is on his way to meet with others who are more spiritually advanced than him. The Four of Cups represents boredom, disappointment, and feeling stuck in a rut. You may feel like you're wasting your life away at home watching television instead of living it, or maybe the opposite – that the world holds no spiritual meaning for you whatsoever, and all you can think about is how much work there is to be done. Sometimes we become slaves to our own minds.

Five of Cups

The Five of Cups shows us five open cups arranged around an empty space, but this time they look different. Rather than being placed flat on their sides, one on top of the other, or upright like flower pots, these five cups are in a curve, so they touch at the top. Like an arch or doorway, they form a sort of portal between their world and our own, but there's no one in it. All five cups are empty except for three small drops of water at the bottom of two of them; all five figures have turned away from us to face this gap instead.

One is even walking into it with his back to us. There are no more dancing figures or smiling children here- just stone-faced men all dressed in grey, which looks very serious indeed. The Five of Cups represents loss, sadness, and regret. Most likely, you've recently experienced some kind of loss that has affected you deeply, whether emotionally or materially. Maybe someone has died, or a relationship has come to an end. The Five of Cups can also mean feeling abandoned or let down by someone. It's important not to give up, even though the cycle is ending, and these men will soon be facing us again as we move onto the next card in the deck.

Six of Cups

The Six of Cups is a bit of an odd one as it doesn't seem to represent any particular event at all. The six cups are set up like the Five, only this time they're arranged two by two on either side of three taller cups arranged in a triangle shape. These "taller" or more advanced cups form a portal, and the Six of Cups shows us another spiritual journey about to begin, or maybe one that's just ended, and we're coming back out through this same portal again. The first figure we see here is an older man with pale skin dressed in light brown clothes, carrying some sort of staff or stick; he's looking backward over his shoulder towards the five cups behind him, which he has just walked through. He looks unsure of himself – these cups are telling him to go back even though he's already walked through them. The second figure is a boy (around ten years old?) dressed in bright red with his hands together as if praying, but he doesn't look like he wants to be here, and it's clear that the older man has chosen this journey for both of them, not just him. The Six of Cups represents having faith or believing in something, hope, and innocence. There may be a child involved in your situation who still believes everything will work out okay, or maybe you're like the old man above, who looks very unsure about making this journey again.

Seven of Cups

The Seven of Cups shows seven open cups all stacked on top of each other, some upside down and some right side up. There are all kinds of symbols floating about in the space above these cups, which represent choices and decisions you may have to make soon. But it's also important to remember that each choice you make will take you down a different path, just like these seven cups. The top three are mostly still full. There are clouds where the water should be, but it is very little or no reflection in them; this could mean that these choices will affect just you, not anyone else around you yet. However, the bottom four are spilling over onto their sides and reflecting everything around them, showing us how the consequences of our actions affect other people. Like the Nine of Wands, the Seven of Cups can indicate feeling torn between several choices or paths ahead in this case. However, there are seven in total.

Eight of Cups

The Eight of Cups depicts eight figures walking away from us, all in gray, except for one who's dressed in red. They're leaving their cups behind, unlike the Five or Six who held these cups even when they walked through. These men have already let go of them, so what comes next won't be based on past mistakes. Several symbols are floating above and around these cups, which may help you figure out why they've left. The tower reminds us of that famous story about a man climbing up to heaven and falling back down to earth. It could represent feeling judged or punished or being too proud to admit when we're wrong. The dog is the only animal in the Tarot deck that can't speak, so he represents our intuition or gut feeling. The angel with one foot on land and the other in the water reminds us of being pulled two ways at once, one side pulling us away from this world while the other pulls us back down to it.

Nine of Cups

The Nine of Cups looks suspiciously like another famous tarot card, the Ten of Cups. Instead of ten cups, there are nine, and these cups are arranged three by three across a lake or river. This time, though, they're all full – nothing is spilling over onto its side.

There's an obvious theme running through these cards that presents itself in each design: life gets messy when you're coming out of a tough experience or flow, but eventually, it returns to normal when you've reached the end. It could be that the previous cup was full to be emptied later. Who says your life is supposed to stay perfect?

Ten of Cups

The Ten of Cups shows us an older couple standing in their garden beside a house, holding hands while watching their children play together in front of them. There are two young children (a boy and a girl), one teenager (boy), and three younger adults (two men and one woman). They're all smiling because they're happy with what they have, and why wouldn't they be? These cups represent everything we could ever want love, family, friendship, etc. The only thing missing here is any representation of money or career. Usually, these are shown by the coins in the man's pocket or the trees in the background.

Chapter 8: The Wands and Fire Signs

The Wands represent the element of fire (also known as the Fiery Signs). They are Aries, Leo, and Sagittarius. These fiery cards have a powerful presence in life and any group setting. Wands will nearly always be part of a person's environment when they feel at home or have found a niche that fits them perfectly. This social prominence has many sides to it since not all wand-people like to be center stage (cardinal), nor do they all take time for personal love relationships (fixed).

The Suit of Wands corresponds to most Tarot decks' "fool" card. The wands represent education and good luck through new ventures and opportunities aligned with our true desires. When this suit is drawn in a reading, it serves as an omen of success achieved by patient passion; excellence can be expected but not without effort. With courage, the seeker can face challenges head-on and overcome them victoriously. The suit of wands also denotes artistic expression, reflecting inspired creativity coupled with uninhibited ideas based on original thought (not a copy of someone else's work).

The seeker can rise above struggles and let opportunities come naturally without getting stressed out over it all. The Wands Suit indicates positive changes within a relationship that will improve the couple's circumstances in romantic readings. When this suit appears reversed in a reading, it signals disappointment. It may also indicate being stuck in situations from past mistakes that haunt or overwhelm the seeker; the burden of wasted time weighs heavily on the seeker's consciousness. The element of water can be seen when this suit appears with cup cards, representing relationships and emotional matters coming into play alongside business matters.

Keywords

Upright: Initiation, movement, action, passion, sexual, enthusiastic, inspirational, personal development, competitive, the thrill of the hunt, growth, careers, business, opportunities, enterprise, optimistic, commerce, proactivity, spirited, spirit, outgoing, energetic, impulsive, vision, spirituality, sexuality, vitality, creativity, intuition.

Reversed: Distrust, sadism, misleading, selfishness, aggression, heartlessness, risk-taking, too much optimism, mean-spiritedness, conniving, manipulation, brashness, hyperactivity, narrowmindedness, greed, ruthlessness, impetuousness, rashness.

Ace of Wands

This is the first card drawn in a spread. You can use this as a key to look at what's happening overall. It acts like the Fool card from the Rider-Waite deck in some ways since it speaks about entering into a new cycle of life right from the start. In reverse, The Ace of Wands brings disappointment in the outcome of a new venture or business idea that will end up being delayed in its implementation. In some cases, it can also indicate starting a new idea only to abandon it quickly in exchange for an older pursuit. This card may represent frustration coming from unfulfilled desires and stopped progress due to indecision and fear of moving forward.

The Ace of Wands brings with it a new start and exciting possibilities that will bring the seeker out of their comfort zone. It may signal that they have successfully sustained an idea for a business over time and now will begin to see the fruit of their labor manifest into something beautiful and rewarding. This card can also indicate finding passion and inspiration in one's work, starting new relationships on equal ground, or not letting hardships hold you back from living your dream life.

The Ace of Wands draws upon the element of fire, which is associated with creativity and passion. With this comes excitement and inspiration that catalyzes future action. The Seeker has already successfully weathered their ideas through testing them out without any negative consequences thus far; this is a good indication that they'll be able to handle whatever lies ahead because their mind is set and ready. The Seeker should use their innate passion as fuel to accomplish whatever tasks they might be facing right now that seem difficult or insurmountable. Even if the Ace of Wands doesn't feel like a direct answer to the question asked, it can still provide insight into what direction the seeker wants to move in – the ace represents ideas, creativity, and inspiration, so we must look at what other cards appear first to get a better idea of what this means for them personally.

When reversed, this card may speak of disappointment and missed opportunities due to the fear of taking risks. It may also suggest procrastination from lack of focus or distraction from secondary matters that take one's goals away from them. For those in relationships, the Ace of Wands reversed may speak of a relationship without much passion or excitement due to complacency or a lack of effort from both partners. In business matters, the Ace of Wands reversed can indicate a project that has been initiated but must be put on hold for now due to other factors.

The ace of wands is related to the element of fire and sparks creativity, motivation, and enthusiasm in the querent. The ace of wands represents a new interest or idea that can grow into something big. The element of fire is associated with the zodiac signs of Aries, Leo, and Sagittarius. When this card appears in a reading, it can indicate a need for the querent to take action in some area of their life or ask for help to do so if it seems they are struggling. When the ace of wands appears in a reading surrounded by other cards, it indicates a need to take action before an opportunity passes by. It can also indicate opportunities in the querent's life or things they have to look forward to that will help them take that first step.

Two of Wands

When the two wands appear in a reading, it represents harmony and balance. This can be seen as an indicator that the querent should take time for themselves, so they don't burn out from taking care of everyone else. It is also a message that no matter what happens or who comes into their life, if they remain balanced and steady, everything will work out fine. However, if the querent feels overwhelmed by all that is on their plate, things may become problematic later on down the line.

The two wands represent future plans and projects that need to be undertaken. This card can indicate a long-term plan or goal that the querent is perfecting. It can also mean waiting for the right time to take action on something they have been planning. When this card appears in a reading, it reminds the querent that patience is needed in their situation. If they are not patient, they may find that things do not turn out as planned because the energy put into the original idea was rushed and unfocused. When surrounded by other cards, it can indicate stability in the querent's life during times of change or when multiple changes are happening at once.

Three of Wands

Drawing this card means that the querent's ideas are materializing and becoming more real. It can indicate happiness or satisfaction with how their life is going at the moment. When this card appears in a reading, it shows that there is still work to be done by the querent in whatever area it represents, but also that they should celebrate what they have already achieved so far. If negative cards surround this card, then it might hint that while the person feels successful now, there could be challenges ahead that will force them to reassess how well their plans are working out for them. When surrounded by positive cards, it can show that the querent's plans are working out well, and they will be able to continue on their path of success.

Four of Wands

The four wands symbolize happiness in a situation that the querent or another person has felt. It can also represent a successful step forward for someone else that is close to them, either emotionally or physically. This card indicates a new stage in a project of long-term importance being reached and celebrated with friends and loved ones. When this card appears in a reading surrounded by other positive cards, it can indicate that there will be many opportunities coming up for the querent, and they should embrace what is offered to them. When surrounded by negative cards, it can indicate that sometimes more of a good thing can be detrimental, and the querent may feel overwhelmed with the level of success they have achieved.

Five of Wands

The five wands symbolize competition or confrontation in multiple areas of life for the querent or another person close to them. This card often indicates that something needs to get done, but others are also vying for this position, so there will more than likely be some kind of disagreement for this goal to be reached successfully. It can also show disagreements within a group working together towards a common goal who are not seeing eye to eye at the moment. This is a challenging card that can signify challenges or problems being experienced in the querent's life. It points to times when someone could be experiencing opposition from other people and their own ambitions and ideas, which could lead to tension between either themselves and another person or two opposing forces (such as their own good intentions clashing with negative influences). When positive cards surround this card, it can show that however hard things may be now, there is light at the end of the tunnel. It can show that these challenges will be temporary and that the querent has what it takes to overcome them. Surrounded by negative cards, it shows that if they wish for change, then they must change something about how they are approaching the situation because things need to change before anything becomes too much for them to handle. There is something that needs doing, but others are also vying for the opportunity, so there will more than likely be some kind of conflict or disagreement for this goal to be reached successfully.

Six of Wands

The six of wands signifies success after having worked hard for something over a long time. It can signify honor or recognition gained when someone has done something well or has completed something they have been working on for a long time. This card can indicate that the querent (or another person close to them) will be recognized or rewarded for their efforts and hard work. When surrounded by positive cards, it can show that this honor or recognition will come quickly and with ease, while surrounding negative cards can indicate that there will more than likely be some kind of conflict or disagreement for this goal to be reached successfully.

Seven of Wands

The seven of wands signifies standing up for oneself against others who may try to harm them or stop their progress, either through direct confrontation or gossiping and badmouthing them. This card often shows that the querent (or another person close to them) will need to defend themselves against others who are working against them in some way. When this card appears surrounded by positive cards, it can show that these challenges are temporary and the querent has what it takes to overcome them. When surrounded by negative cards, it can indicate that there will be more of a struggle ahead for the querent before their success can be achieved.

Eight of Wands

The eight wands represent quick or rapid progress on something that has only recently begun or has occurred unexpectedly. It also indicates someone suddenly making headway on a project they have been working on that has only just come to fruition. It can indicate that the querent (or another person close to them) will have opportunities coming their way quickly, and they should embrace what is offered to them. This card often indicates that something will happen very quickly, and it is a sign of momentum being gained, which is all in favor of the querent (or another person close to them). Things are being initiated at a fast pace where the querent has no control over this momentum, but they should just go with it wherever it takes them as this movement is on their side, even if it feels out of their control. When surrounded by positive cards, it can show that this positive momentum can continue successfully and signify promising new beginnings. In contrast, being surrounded by negative cards can indicate that there is some kind of block or setback preventing progress from being made; something may be being hurried along with more than the querent would like. While some good might come of this situation, there may also be some drawbacks involved.

Nine of Wands

The nine of wands signifies overcoming difficult obstacles to achieve success. It shows valor and courage during troubling times when things do not seem to be going well or when someone is under increased pressure or stress at work or in their personal life. This card often shows that the querent (or someone close to them) will need to be courageous and stand up for themselves during a challenging time. When surrounded by positive cards, it can show that these challenges are temporary and the querent has what it takes to overcome them. Surrounding negative cards, however, indicate that the road ahead is more difficult than it may at first appear.

Ten of Wands

The ten of wands signifies that there is too much work for one person to complete. It indicates burnout and feeling overwhelmed by what needs to be done. This card often shows that the querent (or another person close to them) has taken on more than they can handle at this given moment in time, which eventually leads to feeling overworked, stressed, or burnt out. It represents delays on something that is already difficult enough before things get even harder. It signifies awkward situations arising from too much stress or pressure, making very slow progress. If this card appears surrounded by negative cards, it can indicate that these feelings will last longer than expected. It can indicate that these delays are substantial, and there is more of a struggle ahead of the querent before their goal or dream can become a reality. When surrounded by positive cards, it can show that the querent might need to take a break from their tasks before continuing with everything they have ahead of them. It can also indicate that they (or someone close to them) have great strength and will be able to overcome any setbacks with ease, especially if external factors caused them.

Chapter 8: The Pentacles and Earth Signs

The Pentacles suit of the tarot is connected to the earth signs. This means that the element represented by the pentacles suit is Earth, matching the cardinal signs. Earth signs are also referred to as "Roots," and are Virgo, Taurus, and Capricorn. This suit, which appears in the traditional minor arcana tarot cards, consists of ten numbered cards and four court or "honor" cards, in addition to the usual four suits.

The traditional tarot pentacles are actually coins or discs (disks) or representations of gold coins. "Pentacle" was an early name for this suit, but it is now sometimes reserved to indicate the Five Coins of the Minors. A modern deck may use pentacles, diamonds, or pentagrams as the symbols for this suit.

Disks or pentacles represent safe harbors in the earth element. They also refer to a practical and efficient business and to the foundations of a family. Disks are about your marriage, your home, and your material possessions. They are also about your reputation, your name, and your legacy.

Keywords

Upright: Exercise, fitness, health, domesticity, money motivation, materialism, being down to earth, realistic, dutiful, dull, scholarships, apprenticeships, prosperity, wealth, luxury, growth, fertile, lush, sensibility, groundedness, straightforward, regular, traditional, common sense, artistic, skillful, skilled, practical, stoic, reliable, dependable, lithe, strong, sexual, sensual.

Reversed: Moronic, covetous, greedy, selfish, unforgiving, lazy, penny pincher, thoughtless, superstitious, pessimistic, negative, dullard, shoddy work, neglectful, pleasure seeker, workaholic, slave driver, miserly.

Ace of Pentacles

The Ace of Pentacles in the Rider-Waite tarot deck features a hand coming out of a cloud, holding up a pentacle. It is an earth element card and is numbered "0", like the Fool card that precedes it in some decks. This card is not always numbered "0". In fact, it has a higher number in some decks, such as in the Thoth Deck, where it is numbered 11. There is a human-like figure in the background of this card, with his hands raised to support the pentacle.

Some say that the figure in the background of this card represents God, supporting Adam while he is in a deep sleep. The figure on the card appears to be in the middle of a deep sleep, with his hand reaching out to hold up the earth element pentacle. This card is also known as "The Lord of Material Success" or "Sovereignty."

The meaning of the Ace of Pentacles varies according to its placement in a tarot spread and whether it is accompanied by cards signifying a positive or negative aspect. If this card is surrounded by "positive" cards (such as the Ace of Wands and King of Swords), then it predicts that financial success is at hand. If this card is surrounded by "negative" cards (such as the 2 of Cups and the 7 of Swords), it predicts financial loss. If this card appears in a reading about the querent's romantic life, it predicts that the querent will be involved in a relationship with someone rich and very generous. They may fall into this relationship unexpectedly, or it may have been building up gradually.

This card predicts good health and a long life when drawn in response to the querent's health. In reading about the querent's family, this card predicts that the querent will soon gain an inheritance. It is common for the Ace of Pentacles to appear in a reading as a sign that it is time to focus more on financial success and material gains.

Two of Pentacles

This card is one of the "negative" ones, but not an unattractive one at all. This card is about balance and harmony. The two pentacles balance each other nicely, each side taking its turn being up in the air. Sometimes this card shows up when you need to consider both sides of something. It shows up when you need to find a balance in your life at other times.

The two pentacles could also show that something is out of balance in your life or that you need to bring more balance into it.

This card may also show up if you are trying too hard on one side but not enough on the other. It can even show up when you are so balanced that you have no passion or drive. It can tell you that you are too inflexible with your goals and ideas. Try not to let your ego get involved in this reading. It may also be a sign that something is out of balance.

This card can also show up when you have to work on a partnership between two people. You might need to work on a relationship with a friend, a romantic partner, a family member, or an employer. This card can also show up when you are trying to decide between two different paths, whether that be concerning a job, a romantic partner, a house, a school, or an opportunity.

Three of Pentacles

The Three of Pentacles is often a card of hard work and skill, but it can also be a card of boredom. In the situation you are in, you may feel like you are doing everything you can, but you are not getting the results you deserve. It can signify a situation where you are working hard but not getting paid for it. It can also mean that you are taking on too much, and you cannot give a good level of effort to everything you are doing. You might have bills to pay and be working hard, but you are not getting a paycheck.

Be careful not to overwork yourself. If you feel that you are not getting paid enough, speak up. Play fair with your boss and be honest about what you are willing to do for how much pay. It may be time to move on if you can't get a reasonable deal.

This could also be a relationship that is a lot of work, but you are not getting the romance you want. You may be undervalued or underappreciated. Or it can indicate a situation where you are paying your dues, but you are not happy with the situation. You may feel like you are being used or taken advantage of. It can also be a card of inattention, being too busy with other things to really pay attention to the work you are doing.

But the Three of Pentacles doesn't always represent a negative situation. It can mean that you are in a situation where you are learning and growing. You may learn new skills, grow mentally or spiritually, or even develop a greater understanding of yourself.

Four of Pentacles

Contrary to what many assume, the Four of Pentacles or the Four of Disks isn't about safely stacking your money or being careful with spending. It's about taking steps to make your plans concrete, creating law and order, and having a routine that will encourage you to grow. The card represents the establishment of your ideas. That is the first step towards an idea becoming a real, tangible thing. It is no longer something you imagine or fantasize about but something that exists and can be materialized. You've taken the first step, and you can guarantee its reliability and longevity. This is a very significant step.

The card also speaks of a return to a state of stability and security. Quite often, we don't see that as valuable because we are used to the excitement of change. We see the bigger picture without considering that it is interrelated with the smaller and more mundane picture. This card means a pause, a return to what you know, what you have, and where your roots are.

This card could also mean you're looking for security and stability in your relationship now more than ever. It's important to you, but so is being true to yourself. You don't want to feel suffocated by your lover. You're in a tug of war between giving and taking, and the struggle could create a lot of tension in your relationship. To get out of this pattern, you need to recognize that this is not the end of the world. Sometimes, you need to slow down and assess your relationship. What needs work? What needs to stay the same? Once you start answering these questions, you won't feel pressured to make a quick decision, and you'll be better equipped to deal with the likely stress that comes with a relationship.

Five of Pentacles

The five of Pentacles represent a time of crisis. This is a time to be courageous and remain calm during trying times. It's a time of great financial instability, but other readings have shown that the five pentacles can also be a time of success for a person who is willing to work hard and make the necessary sacrifices to achieve their goals.

The card could indicate a period of great loss and hardship, such as being burdened by debt, divorce, or the death of a loved one. In other cases, it shows that this is a time for a flourishing business and financial security. While it does not dictate success over failure, drawing this card means the time to decide is now.

It is sometimes referred to as the "five of woe" because it is considered to be a card that signifies sadness, loss, and bad luck. It also indicates the loss of a friendship or close personal relationship. It can represent the death of a loved one or someone you know.

If you have drawn this card reversed, it indicates that you have overcome some type of hardship or obstacle. You have addressed and/or resolved the issue to your satisfaction. It can also indicate that help is on its way to you or that something good is about to happen.

Six of Pentacles

The six pentacles are always a very welcome sight, whether they represent kindness and help headed your way, or you see it as you are being the giver of good. In readings, you may be told that a situation may develop where you need to show some compassion or generosity. If you are the benefactor, you need to be ready to help those in need. If you are the one receiving help, you need to be willing to accept it.

No one likes a whiner who doesn't want to do anything in return for the kindness they receive. This card brings with it good fortune and abundance, but it can also be a sign that there is something good heading our way. It can also be a reminder that help is there for you if you need it. This is a card of stability, security, and comfort. The journey is over, and the traveler is being welcomed back home.

It also represents the building and establishment of a home and family life. The key to happy family life is stability and security, with pleasant and comfortable surroundings. When the 6 of Pentacles appears in a reading, it often indicates inheritance, land, property, or financial stability. It often appears in a reading to signify the end of a problematic or upsetting situation and the start of a new, happy, and stable period in your life.

This card is especially important if you seek employment, as it can mean that you will be offered a steady, secure job. The message of the 6 of pentacles is that you can rely on your family and friends for support and that you can make a good living for yourself and your family.

Seven of Pentacles

The seven of pentacles card is about your patience finally proving to be worth it as you receive the reward of waiting for something that's been in the works for a long, long time to manifest at the right time. This card encourages you to sit tight, trust in your hard work, do the right things, and then reap the rewards for the long term. It's about those long-term dreams and goals you've been patiently working towards. Patience is a virtue. Believe in the power of patience to bring you the rewards you seek. This card could also be about being rewarded for your hard work. For example, you may have been working on a business plan for a while, but now it's finally come together. There could also be a delay of sorts. For it to be worthwhile, you'll have to wait a bit longer. Your hard work will be rewarded. The Seven of Pentacles is a card of intention. This card may be telling you that you need to be patient, have faith, and trust in your own abilities. You can manifest what you desire once you put the intention and energy behind the goal. Sometimes, we place obstacles in our own path to happiness, preventing us from attaining what we want in life. You may need to clear any obstacles that may be blocking your path to happiness. The Seven of Pentacles can also indicate mental illness. You may be experiencing feelings of hopelessness and despair.

Eight of Pentacles

With the eight pentacles, you get the message that you're familiar with your daily routine and work. Yet another aspect of the 8 of Pentacles that isn't normally talked about is that it asks us to switch things up and do something different each day, even if it's just a bit. It asks us to get out of the rut we're stuck in and try something creative. It's a card that asks you to set aside some time to do art, write, or think about a creative project that you're really passionate about.

Daily routines and creative outlets are both important, but the 8 of Pentacles asks us to spend some time in each place. You can't expect to find a creative outlet if you've never tried anything new before, and you'll never expand into a new realm if you don't go outside your comfort zone. It's that feeling that you need something a bit different to shake you up, but how can you do that as an adult?

The answer is simple: by being more spontaneous. This doesn't mean that you need to go to Vegas and get married to the first stranger you see (although it's probably a horror movie waiting to happen). But it does mean that you need to step out of your comfort zone a bit and do something that you wouldn't normally do. It's the card that asks us to be prepared to do something that we wouldn't normally do. It encourages us to change our routines. Try to do that in little ways, like taking a different route home and going from there.

Nine of Pentacles

The nine of pentacles says that it's finally time for you to kick back, relax, and enjoy all that you've worked very hard for. You need to take the time to enjoy all you've created for yourself. It wasn't easy to acquire them, so it's justifiable to take time off and appreciate how far you've come. This is not a time to go get more, or be greedy, or to push your luck. The time has come to enjoy what you already have and all you have become. The 9 of Pentacles is a good omen in Tarot. It suggests that your hard work has paid off, and you have reaped the rewards of it.

You may have had to make some sacrifices along the way and put in a lot of hard work. But the fruit of your labor is now clear. You have turned your aspirations into reality, and you have paid off the hard work. The card often appears in the reading when you have achieved an important goal, or it might be in relation to a new business venture. It is telling you that you have a good work ethic and that this is one of your strengths. For balance, you may also need to spend a little time relaxing. It is a good time to take stock of your life and make sure that everything is going as it should. Financially, it can refer to a steady income derived from a reliable job or a steady income from a previously successful business.

Love can be in the air, and this card attracts love. It is also associated with marriage and strong, permanent relationships. It is also a good omen for career matters, suggesting that you will make a lot of money from a job, business, or sale of a property. However, the 9 of Pentacles doesn't necessarily mean it's time to be complacent. It can warn you to be careful and not to take anything for granted, as you might fall back into hard times if you don't keep going with your work.

Ten of Pentacles

The ten of pentacles says there's no better time than now to work on expanding your business, organizing your family get-togethers, and looking optimistically towards the future. Your accounts are flowing with money, you have an excellent support network, and any storm that comes your way, you can handle it with ease. The card also appears when you're feeling stuck in a rut and need to get back on track. It points your attention toward what you've already accomplished and tells you that if you continue on this path, you'll achieve your goals. It is associated with your career, health, and longer-term investments in your life. The only challenge you face is protecting your hard-earned money from being wasted on the frivolous, the useless, or the unnecessary. Absorb knowledge about what's going on in your world, focus on your goals, and make the most of the hard work you're putting in. You're going places, and you need to keep a clear head. The 10 of pentacles in love and relationships is interesting too. You may be faced with the feeling of being unappreciated even though it's clear that you are doing everything in your power to make your partner happy. If you are involved with someone who is either unemployed or underemployed, this card can be a reminder that it may be time to look at new opportunities.

Chapter 10: The Swords and Air Signs

Let's talk about the Suit of Swords. It is all about life's problems and our mental processes. It has to do with how we speak, learn, and write. It rules the world of logic, dealing with intelligence, decisions, and facts, all of which influence our lives. The sword is an instrument of execution, and the two sides of the sword symbolize the brain's two hemispheres. It's also about using intellect and analysis to approach a situation and using the written word and speech.

The Suit of Swords relates to the element of air and could be said to relate to the mind. It represents the intellect, with the Ace being a beginning or birth. It also relates to rationality. It could also be said to represent the higher self, intuition, and the subconscious. The suit of swords in astrology is connected to Libra, Gemini, and Aquarius, represented by the planet Uranus and connected to the Tarot card of Judgment. It is associated with the 8th house in numerology, which relates to death and rebirth.

The Swords is a very active and strong suit, one that is associated with action, motion, and the phallus. It is known as the "suit of the intellect and reason." During the Middle Ages, the suit of swords was renamed the "Coat of Arms." The Swords are also connected to the 3rd eye and the pituitary body.

Keywords

Upright: Definition, facts and figures, thoughts, mentalism, mind, equilibrium, balance, inspiration, ideas, cognition, reason, arguments, disagreements, logic, intelligence, issues, communication, tension, worries, decisions, problems.

Reversed: Bad life changes, issues with mental health, being illogical, biased, mental blocks, confusion, indecision, inertia, accidents, malice, spite, unemotional, cold, manipulative, ruthlessness, viciousness.

Ace of Swords

The Ace of Swords asks you to be open to new ways of looking at things and fresh ways of thinking. It asks you to welcome new perspectives when it comes to how you see and describe the world and your role in it. It's about heightened emotional intelligence, which must be used wisely.

This is the card of spiritual power and divine force. Once you connect with its energy, you can make it work for your benefit, but if you don't know how to harness this energy, it will become your enemy. The diamond shines brilliantly in the center of the card. It is not the past or future, as the card suggests. It is the present moment, and everything that you need is right here, right now. It's about taking responsibility for your own feelings and being aware of the feelings of others.

The Ace of Swords asks you to open your mind to compassion so that you might be able to think clearly and wisely. It asks you to be the calm center of your storm. It asks you to be thoughtful, have empathy, and be sensitive to others. This is a time for the sword of truth. It's a time for you to be "truthful" with yourself and with others. It is the card of a systems thinker, a strategist, a planner, a tactician, and a forward thinker.

Two of Swords

The two swords show you that while things are calm, not everything is okay. You need to take some time to create balance in your life and carefully consider your actions, choices, and feelings. Don't be so quick to say yes to things that you wind up spreading yourself too thin. You can find peace again, but it's still pretty easy to lose it.

This card is about knowing when to step back and regroup. You can do all the work in the world, but you won't see results if you don't take the proper time to rest. You're likely to feel conflicted about your love life right now. There could be a struggle between your present and your future. If you're currently in a relationship, you might be feeling unsure of your partner.

Don't turn your eyes to the past, as this card says it's time for you to stop reminiscing about the past and start turning your attention to the present. It's time to move forward with your life.

Two of Swords predicts that you will be making a big decision over the next month. Despite the fact that it is a huge decision, this card says it's one that you've been putting off for quite some time.

The Three of Swords

This card comes up in readings to show you that you are having a hard time dealing with the pain that has been in your life for so long. But now is not the time to wallow in self-suffering, though. Instead, make sure that you're not turning to things like alcohol or another escape so that you can truly heal. Remember, there is light at the end of the tunnel, and it's important to focus on it. The card says that the healing process may take some time, but if you stay strong and take care of yourself, you can come out of the other side stronger.

The Three of Swords is also a card of abandonment and betrayal. If you are facing a situation where someone has hurt you in some way, be it physically or emotionally, know that things will come around for you.

A love reading can tell you that you may have gotten your heart broken or that someone you care about is suffering due to a breakup or a divorce. The trick is to know that you have the power to change this, even if it feels like you don't.

The card is drawn to tell you that there is a new start about to present itself to you. It may not be easy, and it may not be fun, but in the end, you'll find the love you deserve and live the life you want to lead. You will simply have to push yourself to get there.

The Four of Swords

The four swords are a card of rest and release. You may have felt frustrated and stressed lately, and you may have felt the need to rest. Now the time has come to let go. You may have felt like the walls were closing in on you or that it was all too much. This card is here to remedy all that. Now is the time to detach and turn your attention elsewhere. It is often associated with going on a journey to find yourself and your true path in life.

This card brings the peace that comes after a difficult period in life. It says it is time to put down your burdens, forget about your worries and live for the moment. It is time to sit back and enjoy the peace you now have and appreciate the freedom that comes with it. The card is also associated with taking a break from your life and all that you are involved in, to go and do something completely different. The Four of Swords is a message to lighten up and let go. This card often says, "Don't worry." Let it all go. The rest is coming. Let down your guard and let yourself relax.

The Five of Swords

The five of swords is an unpleasant card that can get very nasty and very personal. It's about those who look to one-up each other, who always have to ignore boundaries and have the last say. With this card, it means someone's going to get hurt, or they're being hurt, and someone else is loving their pain. It's an unpleasant card to throw and an unpleasant card to receive. The reversed version of this card makes things a little better. The relationship is less intense, less personal, but it's still the same, still unpleasant. Someone is still going to get hurt; someone will still score points.

The five of swords is one of the worst cards in the deck. It means defeat, retreat, and competitive isolation. It can be a sign that a friend-enemy situation has ended. It can also mean the end of interest on your part. It doesn't necessarily mean that you lose your job, but it can symbolize the end of a job or a job you hoped to get. It can mean the end of a romance or a breakup. It can also indicate that someone is trying to turn you into their enemy or that you're being forced to choose your enemies. Maybe this person doesn't know exactly how to handle you, so they try to force you into a position. The five swords in a spread can also mean that you're going to have to fight for something, to stand up for yourself. It's not a card you want to see, but it's one you can use to get your game face on and ready for battle.

The five swords may be a final refusal on someone's part, a refusal to talk to someone else. It can mean the end of a friendship, the kind of friendship that involves a lot of personal criticism and competition. It is a sign of change. It means that you have to change your ways and that working with people is no longer going to work. You have to pull away, retreat, and regroup.

The Six of Swords

This card has been said to represent an adventurer, a knight, or soldier traveling a perilous road and strongly suggests that the querent is searching for a better home or situation. This card bears much in common with the Four of Swords, and if this card represents the querent, then they can expect to be traveling soon. The nature of the trip may be mental or physical, but it will require travel in either case. There is little to do but follow the quest. There is also a strong tie with the Ten of Swords, which represents the end of a difficult road.

The end of the journey may be in sight. But unlike the Four of Swords, which often means a journey away from home, the Six of Swords urges the querent to travel toward home or toward a situation or environment more conducive to their survival. The Six of Swords is also well-known as a card denoting illness but does not always indicate severe illness. The card may also simply indicate a general debility or that the querent has been ill for a long time and will not get better soon.

The Seven of Swords

This card is about theft and futility. It's a card that tells a tale of not putting in adequate effort as well as being in a position that allows you to be taken advantage of. This card could mean that you have a habit of throwing in the towel too soon and allowing some other person to swoop in, wrap up what you started, and take all the glory for themselves.

The card is about a missed opportunity, or perhaps that someone has made a poor effort and missed out on the opportunity. The Seven of Swords is a person who has done all the work and received nothing in return. Meanwhile, the thief is the man with the sack, who is free to steal anything he wants. The key to the 7 of Swords is to recognize the sign that opportunity is slipping away or that things aren't going as you thought they would. The card can indicate a swindler taking our hard-earned cash, a needless battle of words that leave scars, a divorce, or a feud. What gets lost? Energy, time, peace of mind, and wealth. Instead of fighting for what you want, you give up and sit idly by as someone else gets what they want first. As the Seven of Swords represents loss, it may also be a message to practice moderation and avoid excess.

The Eight of Swords

The interesting thing about this card is its duality. On the one hand, you want nothing more than to break free from all the things holding you back, and you're able to. On the other hand, just because you can doesn't mean you've tried to. You don't bother. The bonds holding you back aren't a matter of emotion but of duty. You've chosen to keep yourself restrained because you sense it's the right thing to do.

The shackles are not physical – they are mental. You have imprisoned yourself. The pain of the bonds is less than the pain of breaking them, so you stay. They are a little like prisons in this way, or a straitjacket. If the Eight of Swords shows up in a reading, it's time to break free of your own mental constructs. You are dwelling on the past or on the future. You are caught in a loop, a pattern. This can be your own habitual thinking pattern, or it can be a pattern imposed upon you. Either way, you need to break free. It could also mean you are waiting for the right time to break free, and you know that, so patience is warranted. You've got your head in the right place. You're trying to do this the right way. Life doesn't have to be a race.

The Nine of Swords

This card tells you that you've been struggling to let go of past trauma, negative thoughts and emotions, and bad habits. It could be a past event – an echo from the darkness of the past – or something more current that plagues you. It could be a fear of rejection and abandonment that haunts you. When someone draws the nine swords, there's a chance they also deal with insomnia and nightmares, which can make it even harder to let go of what drains you.

These nine swords encourage you to find your place in the world and gain a fresh perspective as well. Otherwise known as the card of fear, it reveals that you are not letting yourself move past situations but instead wallowing in them. You feel trapped in your life, and you don't have the confidence to let yourself move forward. You are afraid of facing the future and the unknown, which is terrifying. The Nine of Swords represents a time when you feel that everything you have worked for has been taken away, and you are left with nothing.

This card tells you to cut off contact with toxic people in your life and stop dwelling on the past. It can be hard to hear, but you need to let go of those holding you back and detach yourself from toxic emotions. Try to sleep and meditate regularly to bring peace to your mind.

Take time to heal yourself and find your place in the world. Rest and relaxation will help get both your mind and your body back on track, so this card can also tell you to take time to relax and recuperate. Even if your schedule is hectic, you can make room for a relaxing bubble bath or time to read a book.

The Ten of Swords

This card tells you that some important part of your life may be coming to an end. It could be a relationship, a job, or something else that is important to you. It is a card of finality, so when you draw it, be aware of the flexibility in your life.

It represents intellect, emotion, and power, and if you draw this card, it could tell you that you are in danger of losing these things. Therefore, it is time to cut your losses. You may be overwhelmed by feelings of sadness and despair. The end of some phases of your life is upon you, but don't feel that you have failed. It is time to let go and move forward. Do not cling to the past but think of it fondly and be thankful for all you have learned and experienced.

If this card appears in your reading, it may be an omen that some important person in your life may be leaving. It may be a relationship that is wearing out or a situation that cannot continue. It can also mean that you will soon be free from that part of your life or situation. However, this card is not always a good sign. If it comes up in a reading, you should consider how much you want to break free from the situation. If breaking free will makes you happy, this card may be a good choice. It seems that now is the time to deal with your past, present, and future. The Ten of Swords is about the harsh reality of life, taking the journey of overcoming, and the initiation of healing. At its heart, it is about moving on with your life. You will feel a sense of relief and a sense of starting anew.

Chapter 11: Your Birth Year Cards

A tarot birth card is a card that has the same astrological sign as you do. This means that your personality is more likely to resonate with the interpretation given for this specific card.

The tarot birth card is one of the most commonly used tarot spreads, and it is often used for past, present, and future tarot readings. A tarot birth card is a card in the tarot spread that represents you. It is a metaphor wherein the tarot cards show the elements of your personality in story form. Just as every birthday has a personality, so does every birthday card. Your birthday card reflects your personality, likes, and dislikes. When you read your birth card, you'll discover your true self. Birth cards are also a great way of learning more about yourself and your strengths.

Birth cards work pretty much the same way as the Zodiac in the sense that they make you feel as though you're a part of something larger in the world. They're meant to help you feel as if you have your own place and your own part to play in the world. They also help you learn more about yourself, and so the more you know about your shortcomings and strengths, the better you'll be able to appreciate all the lovely things that other people bring to the table as well. The birth card is meant to help you figure out the more constant aspects of your state of being. It helps you figure out what was going on energetically when you were born, and you can learn about the rules you're supposed to play, the challenges in your life, either phase or the great potential you have.

How to Calculate Your Birth Card

First, split your birthday into 4 sets of 2 numbers each so that you can add these pairs together. It would look like this: MM – DD – YY – YY. So, let's assume you were born on October 23, 2000. This would be 10 – 23 – 20 – 00.

Next, add these numbers together to get birth card number one. The total based on our example would be 53. As it's a double-digit number, we have to add 5 and 3 to get the first card. 8 is the Strength tarot card.

If you get a double-digit number, you should add those digits to get a single number. In our example, it would be 10+23+20+00 = 53. Add 5 and 3, and you get 8, which is strength.

To get the second birth card, you need to split the first number into a number from the tarot. Since 8 is already accounted for (strength), 8 is the result of 1 plus 7. There's no card number 71, so it would obviously be card number 17, which is the Star.

If the sum of your birthday gives you three numbers, you should add the first two to the last one for the first birth card, and for the second one, reduce that to a single digit. Say you were born on June 21, 1989. You would have 21 + 06 + 19 + 89, which totals 135. To get the first card, add 13 to 5. This will give you 18, which is the Moon card. To get the second card, reduce 18 to a single digit by addition, and you have 9, which is the Hermit.

One exception to all these rules is if your total is 19. In this case, you have three cards because adding 1 to 9 gives you 10, and adding 1 to 0 gives you 1. This would mean your cards are the Sun, Wheel, and Magician. If this is all too confusing for you, you can find free handy tools online to calculate all of this for you automatically.

Birth Chart Combos

World, Empress (23, 3): This tells you your path is about self-actualization. You're meant to collect all the pieces of yourself that you keep apart from one another and bring them together so you can finally find yourself at home in this life or World. On this path, love will light your way. You have to learn to give and receive love, and the Empress will show you how. It is the love you carry within you that will lead you to a life of fulfillment, which will, in turn, bless everyone who knows you.

These two cards share the practice of being in the moment and keeping a clear head. The wreath, crown, and symbols in their hands are signs of high purpose. There's also a concern for elevation in spiritual matters. The contrast between both cards means you can be as passive as you're active, reserved as you're expressive, and formal and personal as needed. The World measures the abundance of the Empress, and the energy of the latter is open, balancing the formality of the former.

Judgment, High Priestess (20, 2): This path is about shattering everything that holds you back. It's breaking free from limitations, allowing yourself to move freely outside of the set modes of thought you're used to or that society has boxed you in, so you can build your own system that works for you (Judgement). Your intuition will guide you along your journey (thanks to the High Priestess), and so you have to learn to trust the voice that comes from within, knowing you will achieve the most important work for you if you do.

These are both about the energy of fresh starts, initiation, and awakening. It's about the finality that comes at the end of certain phases and the boundaries that lie between each level of spiritual awareness. The High Priestess stands before the gate that has the secrets of the world and self. Where Judgement sleeps, she remains awake all night. However, when judgment is awoken, it doesn't ignore the call to strip itself of all the things considered dear and start a new world with a new awareness. Together, these cards are not about the mundane affairs of the world. Instead, they are about transcendence. They cause you to rise above the common and banal.

Sun, Wheel, Magician (19, 10, 1): Just as the birth cards of the Wheel and Magician invite you to make peace with change and adapt to it. You should go along with nature's cycles, mining them for resources to help you along your way. You've come to learn and master the universe's shifts and rhythms (the Wheel of Fortune) while working with your inner creation and manifestation powers to go along with the cycles gracefully and successfully (thanks to the Magician). The Sun offers you contentment, peace, and joy along your journey, and it prompts you to enjoy all the abundance you find along the way.

The Sun, Wheel, and Magician form a triangle, and they are the only triumvirate that exists in all the pairs. The sun banishes all doubt and fear, bringing optimism and joy. It is what powers the world's wheels. As for the wheel itself, it's a restless element that exists to continue to move with no end, being both detached from and involved in the drama of life. It moves from highs to lows, from good to bad, on and on. The magician can manifest things and make them disappear. He can create opportunity and possibility and get rid of them. His intent will drive you to create the reality you prefer.

Moon, Hermit (18, 9): This path is about finding the light in the darkness, the clarity in confusion and uncertainty. The world is about illusions, dreams, and phantoms, which present themselves to you along your way. It is about the hidden aspects of life lurking just beneath the surface. As the hermit, you are a seeker guided by the truth within to find the wisdom you seek.

These cards are about the journey, and the heights of life are their goal. One of these is concerned with the darkness of the path yet untraveled, while the other is concerned with the darkness of certain heights which seem unreachable. Where the Moon is about uncertainty, the unrealized, and the whisper of possibility, the Hermit is about that which is finished and the clarity that comes at the end. The Hermit is full of ambition and is clear about becoming even purer while being of service.

Star, Strength (17, 8): This is a path full of hope. You can choose to be optimistic about everything you encounter in life by drawing on the energy of the star while working with the inner strength you possess. You have the choice to leave sorrow behind and move towards growth and regeneration. This means you have to be resilient even in the face of suffering. Hope inspires your actions, and strength ensures your success.

These are both rooted in the creative motherhood you can find in the Empress. The star in you can see goodness and beauty in life, nature, and yourself, and you trust what you see. Strength is the ability to perceive the power that lies within nature and even within yourself and how to control it and keep it contained as needed. The star is remote and of a cooler disposition while strength may be hot. The star represents the perfection that lies in everything and the inherent goodness in life. Therefore, you're not afraid of anything in nature with this energy. You trust that things will be fine if you let them be, choosing to work with the perfection of nature and not needing to improve anything. Strength is about form and force, and as you know, you can't afford to wield your power too much or too little.

The Tower, Chariot (16, 7): This path is about restoring balance, even when the winds of change blow a little too violently. When you are in the middle of a change that completely shifts your world, the inner sense of balance you have will guide you. The tower is about the destruction of your foundations and all structures that hold you back. This process can be rather ruthless, but it is absolutely necessary if you are going to propel yourself forward down a new path. While this process may feel reckless, it will be under the chariot's guidance within you. You will find success by controlling your impulses and being deliberate about your choices.

There is a fair bit of contrast between these two when it comes to energy, control, balance, war, and solidity. The Tower itself is power in its most tumultuous form, often found in the middle of everything. It's the sudden disruption and upheaval of the status quo. As for the chariot, it's about the constant flow of intention, being able to gather all energies and impulses that compete with each other to emerge triumphant overall resistance and challenges.

Devil, Lovers (15, 6): This pairing involves deep sensuality. The Devil combines that which is beastly with that which is divine, the profane with the profound. In the material world, the Devil is playful. However, constant, pure enjoyment could lead to the enslavement of your soul. Thanks to the energy of the lovers, who love to tame the Devil's animalistic and passionate desires and nature, this makes the horrific beautiful and lovely indeed.

It's the devil's job to separate things, offering every element and being in life the chance to be vulnerable and glorious by being on their own, being incomplete, and yet able to find fulfillment. As for the lovers, they're in all things aware that there are two sides to everything. They are the combination of night and day as they are connected to the moon and the sun. They are there to bring all the opposites together and make them one.

Temperance, Hierophant (14, 5): If these are your cards, your path is one full of guidance. You have the wisdom of the Hierophant to help you find calmness, and temperance offers you peace in all conflict. The combination of both cards is like having two excellent advisors within you. One of them grants you access to knowledge that is old and established. The other offers you the serenity of bringing together all the disparate things.

Both cards are concerned with purity in all action and intention, and they're not particularly at peace with a lack of effort and wrong action. The Hierophant in you makes you pay attention to the voice within you and allows this voice to speak through you as needed. This energy will guide you in all you do, helping you see the difference between right and wrong.

As for Temperance, this card's energy in you combines polar opposites to create a passionate power within you. It helps you be aware of the dangers you might encounter depending on your choices and helps you find the path that is best for everyone. Temperance can help you to bust through all the things that hold you back so you can step into your power at last. When these energies meld within you harmoniously, you will find yourself charismatic, focused, and feeling inspired. You may even attract loyal followers to you. You find it very easy to act, speak, and feel from a place of authenticity so that you can act based on your highest truth.

Death, Emperor (13, 4): Death is the closing of doors and the ending of cycles. This is a necessary process to allow new things to flow into your life. The Emperor possesses authority, power, and structure, which you will need in the creation of the new to bring you security and stability in your new normal. A strong will is necessary to bring about the change you seek.

Hanged Man, Empress (12, 3): This path represents easy and gentle movements even during times of delay. The Hanged Man has made willful sacrifices nurtured by the Empress. While the former decides to remain suspended, the latter offers her love to encourage him to continue to pursue his spirituality.

Justice, High Priestess (11, 2): This is a path that brings together fairness, clarity, and harmony, along with a very deep understanding fueled by inner knowledge and intuition. Both the High Priestess and Justice are related to two different parts of life: the spiritual and the transactional aspects. You are the sort of person who has the deep insights of the High Priestess, which are complemented with objectivity and the ability to make sharp decisions thanks to Justice.

The Sun, Wheel, and Magician (10, 1): This is a cousin of the Sun, Wheel, and Magician birth cards. They're all about the cyclic changes of the universe and the randomness of fate (the Wheel of Fortune), learning how to work together with the manifestation abilities and resources of the magician. Know that each time the wheel shifts, you will do just fine.

PART THREE: Reading the Cards

Chapter 12: Psychic Preparation

Many people like having their fortunes told by a psychic who uses the ancient art of tarot card reading. This has become a global phenomenon that is often used in tandem with clairvoyance for foretelling the future or receiving revelations. It takes three things to have an effective reading with tarot: the query of the seeker, tarot cards, and a psychic to make it work. Without one, the others are impossible. As a result, preparing for a tarot reading is critical. So, here's what you need to do to get ready for your reading.

As a first step, take some time to clear your head and quiet your mind.

This is to let the tarot speak to you in whatever way they see fit. Allow yourself to get over whatever worries, anxieties, and expectations you may have. Negative feelings can only impede your psychic abilities. Your psychic skills depend on your energy, and so does the process of reading tarot cards. As a client, when you're putting out unclear energy, you're sending the psychic a message that they don't need to hear, and that might muddy the waters. Also, if you're a psychic offering a tarot reading, your energy needs to be clear and strong, so you can correctly interpret what you're getting from the cards on behalf of the client.

You'll also want to think about what you're going to ask.

Whether you're reading for yourself or someone else, it's okay to have a lot on your plate right now, but it's important to prioritize. Identify which of your worries are urgent and which can only be addressed by a psychic. Preparing your questions ahead of time will help you get the most out of your tarot reading. This way, you can avoid mental blockages that can cause confusion and terror in your thoughts, or even worse, leave you unable to ask anything that makes sense.

Researching tarot readings is the next step.

Even if you won't be doing the tarot reading yourself, it's still critical that you have a basic understanding of the art. This can give you a better understanding of what you're in for. Your negative thoughts may also be calmed by having all the basic information on tarot card reading beforehand. If you're familiar with the basics of tarot card reading and what tends to happen during a reading, you'll be less intimidated by this unconventional approach to getting answers.

The fourth and last step is to attend to concerns outside of you that may be distractions.

External factors like work, home, and other responsibilities can detract from your appointment with a psychic. Consider taking care of these things in advance so that you don't have to worry about them afterward. There is nothing worse than being distracted by non-emergencies. These distractions will have no effect on your tarot reading's accuracy. When getting a tarot reading, be sure to give it your undivided attention.

When used correctly, tarot cards can be extremely potent. Preparing for your tarot reading session is essential because your full participation is crucial. In addition to preparing ahead of time, you really should prepare both your mind and heart to accept and process what you discover during the session. Think rationally so that you are not swayed into allowing your tarot reading to make decisions for you in your personal life. A tarot reading is merely a tool for gaining direction. It can answer questions, but it can't give you definitive answers; that's up to you.

Awaken your intuition.

Your intuition is necessary when you're performing or getting tarot readings. As the one offering the reading service, you need to make sure you're picking up on the correct messages for your clients. As a client, you need your intuition to help you figure out the true meaning of each card and let you know when the reading doesn't really apply to you or may mean something entirely different from what the reader is sharing with you.

Here are a few ways to activate and hone your intuitive powers.

Meditate and make it a habit.

Intuition can be accessed through practices like meditation. An example of meditation is yoga, which is a movement meditation. The asanas? You can just follow the regular methods. Breath and body mindfulness classes for beginners are available for you to take, so all you have to do is quickly look them up online. For those who prefer something a little less conventional, there is also the option of writing meditation. Techniques exist for getting into the state of observing your thoughts and sensations without judging them. The importance of being receptive to intuitive guidance becomes apparent when you begin to tune into your inner world.

Focus on your physical health.

Body awareness is essential. The term "gut feeling" refers to your intuition. Energy healers are well-versed in the concept of "light vs. heavy." Can you recall a time when you were faced with a choice when one option felt light and the other felt heavy? The most important thing to keep in mind is this. Sometimes, our bodies are considerably more sensitive than our minds, and our instincts can serve to keep us safe. This is different from choosing to take the easy street instead of what your gut tells you is right.

Jot down your ideas.

After meditating, you are more likely to hear messages from the spirit world. There are times when you get these signals even though you're just going about your day-to-day business. You should also write all you can about your dreams. The best way to keep track of this information is to keep a notebook handy. Even if your dreams aren't particularly vivid, you should write them down with all the information you can remember. If you regularly practice this technique, the difference between your thoughts and instincts will be easier to see.

This is a great place to get creative with scrapbooking and other decorative techniques. In some cases, channeling psychic insights onto paper might be accomplished by unleashing your artistic side. On the other hand, if you want to keep a neat and tidy journal, you can do that instead.

Be confident in your own abilities.

Long-term, it's harmful to question your intuition whenever you "think" you are utilizing it. An intuitive answer is not a rational one. You know something will happen when your intuition tells you it will, and then it does. If you continue to dismiss your intuitive nudges, you may slow your progress.

If you aren't always correct when trying to use your intuition, that's perfectly fine. To figure out if it was just a regular thought, or you had assumed it was your gut speaking to you, you would have to keep track of what you got right and what you didn't so that you can figure out the differences between how you feel when you're "bang on" (accurate about something) and when you aren't. This further reinforces the prior argument concerning journaling. Keeping a journal might help you figure out what does and doesn't work for your particular case. Intuition comes in many forms, so trust your abilities and don't be afraid to experiment.

Take your time and be careful.

Your intuition will be hindered by anxiety and panic. An overthinking mind can even hinder you from getting any messages at all. To put it another way, your body can't experience anything but overall unease if you're always worrying.

There could be some blurry moments if you're in the thick of a powerful emotional state. Be careful not to confuse your instincts with your powerful feelings. If you've recently lost a friend or a beloved pet, it's understandable that you want to take a break and relax. Before taking any action or drawing any conclusions, give attention to your emotions and get back into a calm state of mind.

Always keep a tarot deck handy.

A deck can help you read messages naturally when you interpret what the artwork is saying to you. If you're willing to go the extra mile, you can even get ones that don't have keywords. When choosing a deck, make sure you like the design on the cards. If you're looking for a beautiful card but don't feel a strong connection to it, there are plenty of options out there.

Performing one-card pulls daily is a simple exercise regimen. Next, without reading the deck's manual (which is usually included with your tarot set), jot down the importance of each card in your journal. There's no need to compare it to anything in the manual.

For the rest of the day, work with the message you picked up from the card. The evening is a good time for you to go back to the card and the insight you wrote on it and journal about any new feelings that have come up.

Learning to trust your gut takes practice.

Do you feel overwhelmed by the amount of work you have to do? Do not lose heart. Even those with years of practice reading the Tarot still have a lot to learn, so don't let your confidence be shattered as you're only just starting out anyway. Think of it as a fun project, an interesting way to learn trust in yourself. You won't be able to awaken and improve your intuition with just one try. Any sport or talent you want to master takes time and effort. Never let yourself down because you can't practice every day. It's best to go at a steady pace and let things unfold naturally. Patience pays off big time.

Psychic Abilities Exercises to Improve Your Psychic Abilities

Predicting What Will Happen Next

A lot of people think that the future can't be completely predicted because people have free will, but making predictions as a way to improve your precognition skills is a good way to learn. Try the following:

1. Predict the eventual result of a sports match.
2. Before you answer the phone, guess who is calling.
3. Predict a big story that will happen in the next 10 days.
4. Keep a dream journal and write down any predictive or precognitive dreams.

Practice Telepathy

To practice telepathy, find someone willing to be your subject, and send or transmit a color, word, or shape with your mind. Then switch roles with them and see how well you can correctly detect their thoughts.

People also use Zener cards as a way to test their telepathy. If you don't have a partner in crime, you can master telepathy with these cards on your own. Keep the cards in front of you, face down. Then go through each one, writing down your guesses. Then, check them.

You can also use telepathy on people who don't know about it, for example, by telling a stranger to turn their head to look at you. That's okay, and it can be very effective. Just do your best to be ethical and try not to influence someone who doesn't want that.

Use Psychometry

Psychometry is the skill of picking up on psychic vibrations when you read about a physical thing. In a group, this is the best way to do it. Each person should bring a small personal item, then combine them and select which one to read. This way, you'll know right away how close you are to the mark.

However, you can also try out different types of psychometry by yourself. Use a picture from a magazine, website, or newspaper of someone in the public eye. Sit down and concentrate on the picture. Record any thoughts that come to you. Try to get information that you can back up, like where this person was born, whether they have siblings, or where they currently reside. Then you can look at your data and check how close you came to being right.

Practice Seeing Auras

Every living thing has an "aura," and it's a good psychic practice to see how often you can recognize what it looks like. If the person, animal, or plant is standing against a white background, you can do this. If you don't have any willing family or friends, take a quick look around the person, animal, or plant. You will be able to see fuzzy colors that were barely there at first. The more you do this, the easier it will get. Here's how:

Notice energy. Before we can begin reading auras, we must first develop a consciousness of the energy within ourselves. When you're next with someone, pay especially close attention to how you feel about them. Do you sense a call to protect and cherish? Or do you sense an invitation to succumb to exhaustion? Utilize sensation to elicit an honest response from your body and breath. Once you develop an awareness of your physical reaction to another person's energy, you'll be better equipped to deal with all types of people you encounter and come into contact with.

Use peripheral vision. It is uncommon for our eyes to detect auras. Every second, we continually screen and process information, and our vision is impacted by hyper-fast thought patterns. To see an aura, you must fix your focus on a single point for approximately 30–60 seconds, enabling your gaze to soften. While you are staring off, begin to notice the forms and colors just beyond your sightline. Take care not to strain your eyes or you trying to see. This induces anxiety and brings objects in your peripheral vision into focus, thereby messing up the exercise. Maintain a gentle focus and allow your breath to slow down to a steady, deep rhythm.

Consider the color. **Color is the simplest way to discern someone's aura.** To evaluate your color vision, do this exercise in a neutral environment. Bring a variety of colorful objects with you. Put these objects as far away from you as possible in the room. Shut your eyes and concentrate on letting the colors communicate with you. Breathe deeply and then gently open your eyes, allowing for a delicate gaze. Consider a single-colored object and begin to stare through it instead of at it. Mentally note the region immediately surrounding the object from this position. After a while, you'll notice a sheen or a mild tint emerging from it. That is an energetic field. This is the start of the aura reading procedure. As your confidence in reading single colors grows, you will be able to manage multi-colored items.

Now read a human's aura. You're ready to go on to decipher another living being's aura. If you're still hesitant about taking this significant step, you can begin with plants. Plants are still unable to respond and will remain so. However, they are still alive and, hence, can emit a distinct type of energy that you can pick up on. Once you're good and ready to test your abilities on another individual, seek out a person willing to have their aura read. Request that your volunteer stands in front of a neutral background. They should be a little further away than a foot from you.

Then fix your gaze on the wall, not on them, so that the individual becomes a part of your peripheral vision. It will enable you to perceive the field surrounding them in comparison to the background. Gently and firmly, take note of any colors that start to show or other changes that occur.

Having conquered this section of the practice, request that your volunteer move about slowly. Check to see whether you can still perceive the same colors as they move. You may even make this more entertaining for yourself by playing their favorite tunes and seeing any changes in their energy that occur as a result.

Chapter 13: Grounding and Intent

How to Ground Yourself before a Tarot Reading

When you're practicing tarot card reading, grounding yourself is important, and so is your intention throughout the session. It's a good idea to ground yourself at the start of a reading before you start shuffling. Grounding yourself is your way of making sure you are fully aware of yourself and your surroundings and that you're protected from psychic energies from others. Think of it as a way of being sober with the universe so that you can focus more on the tarot reading itself.

Groundedness entails being present in and aware of your body, in this moment, and on this planet. This indicates that you are spiritually centered and integrated with who you are. Grounding restores equilibrium to the mind, body, and soul. A grounded person is in touch with their true spiritual self, and they have a sense of security and stability. With grounding, you feel more connected to the Earth and all of its inhabitants. Your body, your life, and your ability to maintain equilibrium no matter what's happening around you all improve as a result of this practice.

Empaths and those with psychic abilities are particularly vulnerable to other people's energies and emotions, which can have a negative impact on our well-being when we're not grounded. If we are ungrounded, we can even become ill as a result of being exposed to the energies and emotions of others, which can manifest as physical symptoms. Similarly, healers must maintain their grounding while healing others, as an inability to do so can result in us being thrown off balance by those seeking healing.

The Anchoring Tree

Your feet should be flat on the ground or floor as you sit in a chair or on your bed. While it is best to perform this exercise barefoot and outdoors, it will still work if you wear shoes and are indoors. Before you begin, take a few deep, restorative breaths.

Now visualize a large, robust, and healthy tree. Consider the tree's trunk. The trunk is substantial, sturdy, unbreakable, and brimming with knowledge and wisdom. Following that, visualize the tree's branches. They are strong, but they move with the breeze because they are also flexible.

The tree's crown is drenched in sunlight and bursting with new, vibrant green leaves, a metaphor for the growth of new thoughts and possibilities. Now, while visualizing yourself as the tree, notice your feet. They are the tree's roots that anchor you to the earth. Your legs serve as the trunk, solidly built and unflinching, providing stability. Your midsection and upper limbs are strong yet flexible branches. Your mind is similar to the crown of a tree, fully immersed in light and brimming with new ideas. Now imagine tree roots popping up from the soles of your feet and growing deep into the ground and extending outward, connecting deeper and clinging to the earth with greater vigor. Sensitize yourself to the earth's presence as it centers and grounds you. As the roots grow deeper, you will feel them release any stress, anxiety, or bad vibes you may be holding back from the earth to be transformed.

After returning that energy to the Earth, visualize light energy being drawn from deep underground, moving up through your roots, the soles of both feet, your legs, and into your first energy center or chakra (the groin area). Continue drawing more energy up into that center and allowing it to accumulate there until the root energy center is completely filled. You should set an intention that you will use this energy as needed for your readings. You've been grounded.

The best time to do this exercise is in the morning, as it will help you get your bearings for the rest of the day. As soon as you get into the habit of doing it every day, it will be second nature.

Extra Grounding Practices

• Take a barefoot stroll through the grass.

• Wander along the sand, dip your toes in the water, and enjoy the sensation of walking barefoot on wet ground.

• Listen to the sound of water as you relax by the ocean or river.

• Allow the sunlight to warm you as you lie on the grass.

• Outside, rest on the grass and observe the clouds.

• Birdwatching, or simply sitting outside listening to the birds sing,

• Visit a park and simply sit outside and inhale the fresh air.

• Switch off your phone, television, and other electronic devices and simply bask in the peace and quiet.

• Consume something you relish and concentrate on the flavors you detect.

• Plant some flowers.

• Meditation

• Practice yoga

• Enroll in a dance class.

• Exercise or participate in sports.

Setting Intentions for Reading Tarot

Intention refers to the idea or intended consequences of an act, event, or sequence of events. The intention is the thing that drives people, making them do things and say things. Your intention is what you think about before, during, and after the act. What you intend is what you want. What you want is your intention.

Here are some examples of intention:

- When flipping a coin, the dealer's intention is to produce a head or a tail.
- Your intention of flipping a coin is to predict whether it will land on a head or tail.

If you had the intention of flipping the coin yourself, your intention would be to predict the result.

Relating to the Concept of Intention

Think of it as a dedication. When you dedicate your reading, with your whole heart and soul, to a cause, person, or pursuit, what could have been an otherwise "empty" reading can take on a personal flavor with commitment and dedication.

It could be a prayer. If you resonate with this idea, then think of your intention as a prayer to a higher power. It's a way to connect to the collective or universal energy.

Intentions give you purpose. In readings, people often ask about their "why." This is a question about their purpose or what they have to live for. Having a purpose is important. It helps you set your serious readings apart from those who just seek a reading because they are bored. Having a purpose will help you remember the meanings and craft interpretations better.

Setting your intention gives you focus. Setting a goal or intention for your cards is a great way to make sure you're focusing on one area of your life. When you have a lot going on, it's easy to spread yourself thin and make lots of different intentions. This can be overwhelming and confusing. Setting one intention for your cards helps you focus on one specific goal or aspect of your life.

Use intention to have a sense of direction. Sometimes you just never know where your interpretations will lead you. You could start out thinking a reading will be about one thing, but it can quickly take a turn and become something else. Intentions will help keep you on track. We all know there's more than one way to skin a cat. Likewise, there is more than one way to interpret a reading. Before you read, decide on the "direction" of your reading. That is, pick which points or aspects you want to explore. Afterward, review your reading with the intention of how it complies with your original thoughts. This will allow you to explore more facets of the text and consider possible meanings.

Now let's talk about the importance of knowing your intentions before you perform a reading. The intention is extremely important when reading tarot. It is important to know your intention before you start the reading because your intention will guide you as you interpret the cards.

For instance, if you are reading for someone you love but feeling angry, then your anger and negative feelings toward that person may come through while reading, making the reading inaccurate. If your intention is to find out about a relationship issue you are facing, the cards you draw may tell you about an ex-boyfriend or girlfriend who will come back into your life.

If you are trying to find out about your career, the cards may show that you will be receiving a promotion at work. Whatever your intention is, the cards will reflect that intention. Unfortunately, many readers do not know their intentions before they begin reading. So, it is very important to have a clear intention before a reading.

There are mainly three areas you can focus on when you are reading the cards for yourself or others when it comes to intentions.

- Will you be reading for the general public?
- Will you be reading about the person's career (work), health, or love life?
- Will you be reading about a specific issue they are having?

You should focus on your own intentions and feelings before you start a tarot reading so you can focus on the energy you are bringing to the reading and really tune into the energy and needs of your client. The three most common interests are love, money, and career. When they ask for a tarot reading, most people are looking for answers to one of these three things.

The intention will be your focus as you choose where to position yourself, shuffle the cards, fan out the cards, and how many cards to draw. It will also guide you as you are interpreting the cards. When you are performing the most basic reading, you will be taking an entire deck of 78 cards and interpreting each card's meaning. That is a lot of information coming at you.

You can set your intention in several ways:

1. State it to yourself. This method is fine, but it is not particularly helpful because you can be consciously aware that you have an intention and still get distracted and start veering off of your original path.

2. State it to the deck of cards and the universe. This method is much better because you are asking the cards and the Universe to help you manifest your intention, so your intention can be more focused and clearer.

3. Write them down. You can write them on a piece of paper before reading and keep that paper nearby so that you can easily refer to it to keep you on track.

4. Meditate to set your intentions before the session.

5. Set your intentions while shuffling the deck or picking the cards.

6. Say it out loud.

7. For five minutes, repeat an affirmation.

There are no right or wrong ways to state your intentions. The important thing is that you set your intentions before the tarot reading begins.

Once you have set your intentions, your interpretation of the cards should fall into place. Your intention will help you determine which cards to choose as you lay out your spread. And once you get your spread, your intention will help guide you to the right interpretation of the cards.

If you don't know what your intention is, then you are likely to end up missing a lot of important information, and you may quite possibly misinterpret the cards.

Emotion vs. Intention

Don't let your emotions get in the way. This can be so easy to do. Sometimes we see a card, and it triggers a strong emotion. Other times, we may not have a clear answer, and we jump to a conclusion because it feels like the only logical outcome.

It's important not to let your feelings dictate your interpretation of the reading. That's like saying, "I know this isn't what I want to hear, but it's what I feel." Take a moment to center yourself. Get some air. Take some deep breaths. Remember why you're trying to get an accurate reading. Then re-read the question, set your intent again, and lay out your spread.

Divine Guidance with Intention

Ask the universe to guide your hand and when you find the card you want, stop, and pull all the cards in that direction. You can also ask your spirit guide to help you, and when you find the card you want, stop and pull all the cards in that direction. Regardless of how you decide, the intention will ensure that you focus on the card and its meaning.

The Problem with Not Setting Intentions

If you have no intention or don't have any particular question in mind, it will be hard to come to a conclusion. If you aren't focusing on a particular question, you may be too focused on yourself and your perspectives. If a tarot reading is done with no intention in mind, you won't get much out of it. The purpose of doing a reading when you do not know your intention is to get a feel for the cards and see what they might be saying to you.

Tarot readings are very spiritual and require a sense of intuition to work. Sometimes, instead of just asking yourself what you want, you have to "prod" the subconscious so that the desire can reveal itself. This is especially true with intentions. You can't always know what you want when you first ask. Sometimes your answer only reveals itself after some mental gymnastics, physical shuffling, and creative, emotional work. The results from starting intention-free can be worth it every now and then.

The Takeaway

And remember, if you want the tarot cards to answer a specific question, make sure you have your question clearly defined before starting the reading and setting your intention.

Tarot cards can be a lot of fun to play around with. But they are also a helpful tool to look at the big picture of life. Setting an intention can vastly improve your tarot reading skills.

What if you don't know what you want? If you don't know your intention, you can always try to guess. Change your intention each time there is a new card or try for a general idea like "What do I need right now?" and see what comes up.

Chapter 14: Seeing Through Card Combinations

In a tarot reading, there are many possible combinations. You can quickly interpret these combinations by examining their relationship with each other and their shared meanings. When combined, the cards will strengthen and support each other in a variety of ways. When a tarot card is combined with another within a reading, the context of the reading, the spread, other cards, and the reading technique will affect how you interpret this combination. There are a lot of factors to take into account when interpreting a Tarot card combination. Because there are over 3000 possible combinations, it's not possible to learn a different reading for each one. However, there are certain techniques you can use to help you figure out what the story is behind the cards.

Interpreting Combos Using Keywords

When reading Tarot cards, there are often several meanings for the combinations. The easiest way to produce an interpretation is by using phrases or keywords. For example, suppose you have two wands (indicating work) and five swords (indicating conflict). In that case, you could interpret this as working with a devious person or about to have a conflict with a work colleague. Another example is having the six cups, which represent childhood friendships, and the eight wands, which represent travel. This could then mean you will travel to meet a childhood friend. Another combination could be getting the eight pentacles which refer to building skills, along with the high priestess, which is connected to intuition. This could mean you're going to develop more intuitive skills. If you like, you can also mix and match the key phrases that you normally connect each card with until you get a combination that strikes a chord within you or your client if your reading is not for yourself.

Interpreting Combos Using Numerology

The fool card, which is the only card without a number on it, can be read with paired cards to discover its meaning numerologically. The number of the paired cards can provide significance to the combination. For instance, if you have two pairings with the same number, the significance of that combination is stronger. For example, if you have the Two of Cups (new relationship) and the Two of Wands (working or partnership), then that means there is a partnership in work or career and love. You also want to be aware that the cards happen to be on the negative or positive of one another. When the cards fall within a range of 1 to 3, this means a new cycle is starting. A range of 4 to 6 tells you that you're in the middle of a cycle, while a range of 7 to 10 implies the end of a cycle.

In terms of numerology, the numbers 1 to 9 are all that matters, apart from the master numbers 11, 22, and 33. The following are the keywords for each number:

1 - Strength, creativity, independence, passion.

2 - Influence, intuition, charisma, trust.

3 - Optimism, charm, attraction, extroversion

4 - Loyalty, discipline, organization, dependability,

5 - Restlessness, free-spiritedness, adventure, loving.

6 - Compassion, kindness, peacefulness, support.

7 - Sensitivity, quietness, introversion, intuition.

8 - Ambition, practicality, hard work, diplomacy.

9 - Spirituality, fighting injustice, nurturing, help.

11 - Empathy, spirituality, psychic, inspiring.

22 - Visionary, wisdom, humility, old soul.

33 - Harmony, balance, self-actualization, integrity.

You can add the numbers of the cards and reduce them to a single digit. If they add up to the master numbers, don't reduce them further. Intuit the connection between the numbers and the card, and you will have more depth in your reading.

Another example could be drawing the Empress (number 3) and the Ace of swords (number 1), representing the start of a new cycle.

It could specifically be about a thought or an idea that's manifesting. The Empress is heavy with the new idea and is ready to give birth to it so it can exist in the world. If you notice that the numbers on the drawn cards aren't close to each other, it could mean that you're moving from one phase to another. If there's an increase in numbers with each successive card drawn, that means progress. If it's a decrease, it could indicate regression. Usually, the tarot reader will work from left to right to figure out the order of these cards.

A final example would be having the eight cups and the two cups, showing how a relationship is developing. It could be that in spite of having a beginning that seemed very promising (on account of the Two of Cups), eventually, both partners could decide to go solo (because of the eight cups). If you were to swap the order of the cards around, the story would be flipped on its head. It would mean that a relationship that has already been developed (8) is turning into something newer or entering a new and deeper phase (2). It could also be that the end of your relationship is a good thing that is making room for a new partnership to blossom. It could also mean that if your relationship is struggling, things are finally about to improve.

Interpreting Combos Using Symbolism

The symbols on the tarot cards can help you interpret the cards according to their themes. Tarot cards hold symbolic meaning. If two cards share a color or symbol, it may tell you something about them. For example, if judgment (which has an archangel) is combined with temperance (which also has an archangel), it could mean that your angel or guide is watching over you or that you are hopeful during a tough time. Check out the meanings of the symbols on the cards to interpret the cards accordingly.

Symbols carry meaning. The personal meaning of the symbol is what you get based on your past experiences. If you don't find a common symbol, then use another method to figure it out, or use your intuition to find the past experiences you've had that may be bubbling up to the surface on account of the symbols shown on the card.

Interpreting Combos Using Elements

There are cards in the Minor Arcana that are straightforward to decipher based on their elemental suit. The suit of Wands belongs to fire, the suit of cups is water, the suit of pentacles is connected to the earth, and the suit of swords is air. The energy shown in a combination of cards with the same element is amplified. However, if the cards have different components, you should interpret them within the context of each other. Here are two illustrations: The combination of the Eight of Pentacles and the Three of Pentacles could indicate a focus on the material gain at the expense of emotional well-being. Here's another one: Say you draw swords, which represent air, and cups, which represent water. This could mean your head and heart are finally finding common ground with each other. If you draw airy swords and fiery wands, this could represent very intense masculine energy, as both of these elements are masculine. The combination could mean turning ideas from wands into action using swords.

Interpreting the Interactions of the Card Characters

There are many ways that people practice tarot card reading. Ideas include in-depth interpretations of each card, in-depth analyses of each position, in-depth analyses of each position combined, or in-depth analyses of the entire deck. If you can't decide which technique to use, try them all for five minutes every day. When you practice every day, you will become an expert at interpreting tarot cards and deepen your readings with additional layers of interpretation. Pay attention to how the people in the cards look at each other. If they are looking away or facing each other, this means something about the relationship. For instance, if you draw the Queens of Cups and the Page of Wands, you could conclude that it's about a teenage boy ignoring his mother. If you draw the Page of Wands and the Queen of Cups, this could mean a deeply loving relationship between a son and his mother.

If you notice that the combination of cards you've drawn involves the characters looking to the right, this could mean that there is a focus on your future. If both characters are focused on the left, it could mean that you're reflecting on your past, for good reasons or bad ones. When the characters are looking forward, this could tell you that you're taking on your problems head-on. However, if they're standing with their backs turned towards you, this could be a sign that you're not paying attention to the present moment and you're seeking ways to escape. Allow yourself to have fun connecting with your intuition, analyze these characters' positions, and figure out what it means to you.

Interpreting Court Cards

Court cards are difficult to understand, but they're also the most important cards in the deck. They can represent people, personalities, or situations involving a person. When you're first starting out with tarot cards, don't overcomplicate them by trying to map out all their possible meanings. The best way to start is by associating each court card with the personality type it represents. For example, if you are your own court card, your personality type is dominant in the relationship. If you are in a relationship with two court cards, then both dominant personalities are important to the partnership's success.

Say you draw the Queen of Wands and the King of Swords. This combination could therefore refer to the process of a woman who is self-assured and confident speaking or interacting with a man who is in a position of authority and very dominant.

You should also be aware of the position of the court cards. For instance, if you have drawn 2 pages, or a king and a page, this will tell you about your maturity level, stage of development, and balance of power. As another example, assume that you drew the Page of Wands and the King of Pentacles. This could imply a partnership between a young apprentice and a businessman with experience. If you draw the King of swords and the page of cups, it could be about the fact that you are ready to take action based on the fresh burst of creativity you have.

Interpreting Majors and Minors

The major arcana cards have different tales to tell compared to the minor arcana cards. So, take a look at the cards you draw to see which group they are from, so you know if you're dealing with a major concern in life or something that's only temporary. When you have drawn two major arcana cards, you need to pay attention because you're likely dealing with a major theme in life or a karmic lesson you must learn.

For instance, let's say you draw the High Priestess and the Hermit. This could mean you're going through a time of serious introspection where you search your soul because you yearn to connect on a deeper level with your higher spiritual self or the Divine. If you pull two cards from the minor arcana, that tells you whatever you're dealing with will not last. Now let's assume that you got the page of cups as well as the three pentacles. Together, these could signify the process of being a mentor to a youthful, creative person. When you have one major arcana card and one minor arcana card, the major refers to the why or what you're dealing with, and the minor tells you how to deal with it. Say you draw the High Priestess and the Three of Wands. This could refer to your connection with your intuition (the what) on a deep level by working on a vision for your future (the how).

Strengthening Versus Weakening Interpretations

There are certain cards in the tarot deck that can be very polarizing. In other words, when you draw these cards, all of your attention is instantly heightened. One of these cards is the Devil. Yet another dramatic card is the Tower. Then you have the good cards that are also extremely optimistic, like the Star and the Sun. It is important to keep your eyes open for these really positive and negative cards. When looking at tarot combinations, remember that they can either weaken or strengthen the combination you draw. However, you should always keep in mind that the cards are neither completely positive nor negative, and so in the light, you will find darkness and vice versa with every card. When the cards you draw are mostly negative or mostly positive, that tells you that the energy is being strengthened. For example, let's assume that you drew both the sun and the star. This would imply that you have huge success in whatever endeavors you're focused on. However, drawing the devil and the tower could imply that you should expect dire consequences because of your addictions. If you notice that one card is very positive and the other is very negative, then that could mean that the energy of both of them is weakened. Or, to put it more accurately, the energy is balanced. This combination lets you know that a situation is not entirely good or entirely bad. A good example of this is drawing the sun and tower cards, which would imply that there could be a blessing in disguise in your life.

Interpretations Based on Being Upright or Reversed

You can also interpret the combinations based on whether they're upright or reversed. When you notice that the cards you've drawn are both upright, this tells you that there is an easy flow of energy and that there's a lot of activity happening in the world outside of you. For instance, when you draw the nine cups followed by the Queen of Swords, and they're both upright, that tells you that you are making decisions that will benefit the collective.

However, if you draw the nine cups and the Queen of Swords and they're both reversed, that could mean that you are content with the decisions that you've made on a personal level. Another interpretation of drawing combination cards that are reversed is that you may be experiencing blocked energy, or there may be a lot more going on in your inner private world. Assume that you drew the nine cups reversed along with the Queen of Swords reversed. This combination in this sequence could mean that you are not content with the decisions you've made for your personal life, or it could also mean that you feel content with your decisions. As you can probably tell, this is very subjective.

Interpretations Based on Flow

Another excellent way to interpret tarot cards is to think about the flow. This is a very subjective method, to be sure. It's all about connecting with your intuition to seek out the symbols, themes, and people common to these cards and noticing how they move, flow or evolve from one card to another. The first thing you should focus on is finding a symbol or something that is common and shared by two cards. This could be the background, a person, an item, or some color. It could also be a theme that embraces both cards. The next thing you need to do is pay attention to the way the theme, color, or shared symbol flows from one car to the next one and figure out what that tells you on an intuitive level.

For instance, let's assume that you drew the Ten of Cups and the six of cups. You noticed that both of these cards have children in common. The former card has the children dancing next to their parents happy. In the latter, they're playing happily as well, but their parents are nowhere to be seen. You could think of this as children growing up, or it could be increased independence while retaining an air of youthfulness and play. Yet another example would be drawing the page of cups and the Sun. You'll notice that both of these cards have flowers in common. In the former card, you will notice that the flowers are on the tunic that belongs to the Page. On the latter card, the flowers are above the wall, and you can see them appear around the head of a young child. You could interpret this to mean that you are taking something that you used to hold very dear to you (the page of cups), and you're choosing to make it a public thing or like the sun. Now, when you've made these visual interpretations, you can go ahead and add nuance by considering the meaning of each card on its own. It's up to you to also consider numerology if you want to. Color is also another important element when it comes to interpreting the meanings of card combinations. If most are the pages of cups and the sun, it could mean that you're finally going to take your art, which you kept private, and make it public. Not only that, but it could also mean that this action will lead to immense success.

Chapter 15: Astrological Tarot Spreads

This chapter discusses casting the natal chart tarot spread by working with the tarot's major arcana and your astrology. Did you know that reading your own birth chart can be a great way to get to know your horoscope better? Even if you're already aware of what your chart looks like, it's still worth consulting with an expert astrologer. Professional readings are always the best, but if you're too intimidated, I recommend exploring it on your own.

A birth chart can be overwhelming, but let's focus on a few of the most prominent aspects. The signs of the Zodiac are the qualities that play out in our lives. Certain signs are emphasized in our charts more than others, but we contain all of the energies in some form. The signs with the most planetary bodies in them, as well as those with your Sun, Moon, and rising point, will have the greatest influence on who we are.

The Major Arcana of the Tarot is comprised of 78 cards, and they highlight potential turning points in your spiritual development. The weather events and cycles of your life and changes that are gaining traction are more important than whether or not you should or shouldn't do something or predict what will or won't happen in the future. Although you have no control over the weather, you can prepare for it and make plans accordingly.

It's the same with the Major Arcana. You can't control their dramatic energies as they pass through, but you can still be cognizant of them and show up in a way that matches the flavor of the present rather than working against it.

A journey through the Major Arcana, which is represented by the numbers 0 to 21, takes us from taking a leap into the unknown to knowing who you are in the universe, who you are as a spirit, and ultimately, how you are connected to something greater.

With each Major Arcana card comes a connection to each of the 12 zodiac signs, or one of the ten planetary bodies acknowledged in modern astrology as being associated with it. Tarot cards can be used to recreate our natal or birth chart, which allows us to gain a different point of view – on both cards and our charts – because of these representations.

Let's take a look at how you could use the Major Arcana to create a tarot spread for personal growth based on your birth chart. I always suggest getting a birth chart reading from a highly qualified astrologer at some point in one's life because it takes knowledge and expertise to read a birth chart correctly. This exercise is not intended to replace a professional natal chart reading, but it is a great opportunity to explore your chart yourself if you are already familiar with the information contained within it.

Signs, Planets, Houses

Astrology is divided into three categories: signs, planets, and houses.

A birth chart can contain a plethora of information in the form of signs and angles, but for the purposes of this article, let's concentrate on a mixture of three systems that work together.

The characteristics represented by the zodiac signs manifest themselves in our lives. Certain signs are more prominent in our charts than others, but we are made up of a collection of all of the energies in some manner. The signs that will have the greatest influence on our personalities will be those that have the greatest number of planetary bodies in them, as well as those that comprise your Sun, Moon, and Ascending Point, in particular.

There are a total of 12 signs. Each of the planets represents a different aspect of our individuality. They can have a variety of appearances and flavors based on the sign and house they appear in on your chart, respectively. In the case of Mercury, it reveals how we interact – Mercury in Cancer appears very differently from Mercury in Sagittarius, for example. The Moon provides us with awareness of our emotional and physical requirements. Once again, the sign and house in which the moon is located will provide us with specific insights into how we should be treated and how our emotions will manifest themselves. In astrology, there are a total of ten planets, which include the Moon and the Sun.

The planets and signs contained within the houses represent aspects of ourselves that we embody in various facets of life represented by the planets and signs. There are a total of 12 houses. So, when we combine all three factors (for example, Venus in Scorpio in the 5th House), you begin to see the nuances and individuality of your public persona and experiences mirrored in your birth chart for the first time.

Placing a pin in this three-part combination will help us remember where we left off when analyzing our tarot spread.

How to Make a Tarot Spread Based on Your Birth Chart

First, locate your birth certificate or natal chart.

Your birth chart can assist you in identifying the links and subtleties that are entirely unique to you and your family. Your horoscope is a map of the sky at the time of your birth that reflects many areas of life and personality, including areas of potential and development.

You'll need to enter your birth date, time, and location information. Even if you don't have the time, you can still get a lot of information about which planets are in which signs by looking at a less accurate chart (which will have erratic rising signs and house placements). There are a variety of free apps and websites available to help you figure this out quickly.

You can start working on the chart once you have completed the drawing (which should resemble a wheel). It starts with your rising sign and the first house, which is positioned at the 9 o'clock position on the chart. From there, the houses are arranged counterclockwise (with the second house at 8 o'clock, the third at 7 o'clock, and so on).

Remove the Major Arcana cards numbered 0-21 from your deck.

This spread will only necessitate the use of the majors. Before you begin, take a look at the planetary and zodiac connections listed below; some of the cards may astound you, and the ordering is not what you'd expect:

- Uranus, the Fool
- Mercury, the Magician
- The Moon, the High Priestess
- Venus, the Empress
- Aries, the Emperor
- Taurus, the Hierophant
- Gemini, the Lovers
- Cancer, the Chariot
- Leo, Strength
- Virgo, the Hermit
- Jupiter, the Wheel of Fortune
- Libra, Justice

- Neptune, the Hanged Man
- Scorpio, Death
- Sagittarius, Temperance
- Capricorn, the Devil
- Mars, the Tower
- Aquarius, the Star
- Pisces, the Moon
- Sun, the Sun
- Pluto, Judgment
- Saturn, the World

Using your chart, arrange the cards for each zodiac sign in a circle around the circle.

Place the Hierophant card at the 9 o'clock position in your first house; if Taurus is the sign of the first house in your birth chart, set The Lovers card, which represented Gemini in the second, followed by The Chariot, which represents Cancer in the third, and so forth.

In your chart, place a card for each planet beside the zodiac sign or card it is occupying at the time.

So, if your Mercury is in Aquarius, you're in luck. The Magician should be placed beside the Star card. Saturn in Scorpio represents the world after death. Jupiter in Pisces is represented by the Wheel of Fortune card, just next to the Moon card.

Take a photograph and write it down.

Because there is a lot of information in this reading, you may need to break it up into several sessions. Take a picture of it so you can easily refer to it later if needed.

With that said, you are free to go as in-depth or as brief as you wish. However, stop to consider the various themes that emerge when you line up the house, the card for the astrological sign residing in that house, and any planets residing in that house.

Some houses will be devoid of planets, which is a nice touch. Then you're just looking at the complex interactions between the house/area of life in your chart and the zodiac symbol that rules that house/area of life in the chart of someone else.

Strength (Leo) rules my Second House of resources, values, and security; there is also The Tower (Mars) plus The Sun (Sun) as well as The Magician (Mercury) in the house. For example, this experience and journey can be interpreted in a variety of ways, both in terms of card definitions and astrological signs and signs and stars. Justice (Libra) rules my Fourth House of home, family, and roots, but there are no planets there, and I can still learn a lot from that combination of signs.

For your convenience, here are the houses and what they represent again:

1st - Oneself, one's identity, one's style (Aries)

2nd – Assets, values, safety, and possessions (Taurus)

3rd - Communication, schooling, mental skills, and siblings (Gemini)

4th - Home, relatives, roots, and one's own inner self (Cancer)

5th - creative expression, enjoyment, and children (Leo)

6th - Work, rituals, health, and routines (Virgo)

7th - Partnership, marital, and the shadow self (Libra)

8th - Sexuality, death, recovery, regeneration, change, and inheritance (Scorpio)

9th - Philosophical exploration, adventure, and innovative learning (Sagittarius)

10th - Responsibilities, reputation, recognition, professional advancement, and public life (Capricorn)

11th - Social life, groups of friends, hopes, and objectives (Aquarius)

12th – Fears, dreams, mystical life (Pisces)

Pause to consider what these configurations of House-Sign-Planet (s) represent for you, as demonstrated in the cards. What have your previous interactions with them been like? What do you have planned for the foreseeable future? When you look at your personal blueprint, what are the connections and unique permutations you can use to help you in the long run?

Sample Reading

Emily had been adopted at eleven months old, and she was looking for anything that might help her learn about her early life. She found most of the information she wanted was unavailable to her, and this frustrated her. Emily was considering legally pursuing access to the records in an effort to learn more about her birth mother's identity and medical history. With this in mind, she decided to come for a reading.

Three of Swords was drawn, showing the root cause of the situation is heartbreak and loneliness. This card displays the pain that Emily must have felt when she was separated from her birth parents at an early age. Despite Emily's foster family taking care of her, the pain in the three swords – the birth parents and baby Emily – piercing their hearts suggests a deep, familial pain.

Betrayal is a very important theme as well because somehow, Emily senses she's been betrayed by many. She has been betrayed by the parents who adopted her and who haven't let her pursue her search. She has been betrayed by an agency that isn't doing what it should. Her birth parents have also betrayed her and, subconsciously, she bears some resentment toward them for leaving her. All these court cards showing up suggest that she has to find balance.

Having drawn the Cups and Pentacles pair, this could represent the desire Emily has to dream about her future (cups) and her desire to remain realistic about her feelings (pentacles). Over the coming months, this theme will prove to be a dominant one for Emily. Page of Pentacles demonstrates that she must pay attention to the more practical aspects if she's going to succeed in her case and discover the truth about where she is from.

From the Knight of Cups, we learn that she tends to be unrealistic about how finding her birth mother will play out for her. This card makes it clear that Emily isn't the best at regulating her emotions and that she has overly romanticized the idea of finding her mother, so much so that her hopes may be dashed. The Queen of Cups was the fourth card drawn, and it reinforces this idea, bringing to mind the concept of "mother." You could refer to the queen as the quintessential mother Emily hopes to meet. She would love for this mother to be tender and loving toward her. This desire is from her past, and it pushed her into the situation she finds herself in right now.

There's also the King of Swords as her seventh card and the Knight of Pentacles as her eighth. The King of Swords points to the fact that Emily thinks of herself as the purveyor of truth and justice in this matter, as she believes she has the right to know the truth about her very first year on this earth. Interestingly, a week before she had this reading, she had crafted a position paper to present to the court. She had relied on the skills of the King of Swords, which include writing, intellect, and analytical abilities.

As for the Knight of Pentacles, he offers a clue that Emily has to be careful about being inflexible. Instead, she should opt to remain reasonable and moderate her emotions throughout this process. Then there's the Five of Cups, which was the ninth card drawn, offering a key to the entire conundrum. It's a card representing loss, beginning with the fact that she had lost her birth parents. It shows that she has to be open to losing the idea of a dream mother, regardless of who the woman is. It's also a sign that Emily is afraid of losing her case.

The Eight of Swords is a clear indication that Emily will likely encounter some confusion in the future. Sometimes she might feel overcome with a feeling of powerlessness, attempting to bring balance to the conflicting emotions she feels within herself. It could also be that she will encounter forces outside of herself doing their best to keep her from getting the object of her search. However, as she drew the Six of Wands as her fifth card and the Magician as the tenth, this showed there could be some positive news for her in the end. The former demonstrates the fact that Emily believes she can surmount all difficulties along her journey and that she will come out victorious. She knows that she will get the victory, as shown by the Magician, the one major arcana card drawn during her reading, showing that there is power backing Emily up that will help her attain her goal. All she has to do is first accept that there will be some loss along the way and that she must rally all her inner strength. When she does these things, she will find great success.

Chapter 16: More Tarot Spreads

Beginner Spreads

We're starting with the simplest spreads for beginners:

- The One-card tarot spread
- The Three-card tarot spread
- The Yes/No spread

The One-Card Tarot Spread

What is a one-card tarot spread? This reading is based on a single card from the tarot deck. It can be done for a person, a problem, a question, or even a quandary in life. While it isn't as thorough as a three-card tarot reading, it's a good way to get a basic idea about what is going on in your life. What can you learn from one tarot card? A tarot card can be a helpful piece of the puzzle when you're trying to gain insight into a situation.

When you pull a single card, you'll be able to tap into the deep, rich symbolism of tarot. That beautiful visual depiction of a card and the story it tells will directly connect to your current situation and the questions you have for yourself. Some people have trouble getting a clear reading off of a standard three-card spread or a five-card spread. If you're just beginning to learn to read tarot, you might have difficulty interpreting the cards you draw, especially if they don't seem to be saying anything right off the bat.

- **Set your intention**. Okay, so you're ready to read from a tarot deck. Before you get started, tune into your body and mind. To start, do a one-minute body scan, breathe some deep breaths, or just find a quiet place to ground yourself. You can also call on any spirit guides, goddesses, gods, your inner being or higher self, or any other divine force you look to for guidance.

- **Ask your question and select your card**. If you want to pick a card from the deck, consider your question. Shuffle the deck with your question in mind. When you feel the pull to stop shuffling, pick a card and turn it over. Take your card from the bottom, middle, or top of the deck – it doesn't matter if it feels right, as long as it's what you wanted.

- **Pause and reflect**. Make your card choice, lay it flat on the table, and don't look for another one. The card is coming up for you for a reason, perhaps especially for reasons that don't make sense to you right now. Just trust it. Journal about the meaning of the card you drew. What does that card bring to mind for you? Personal connections are always worth noting. As you look at the card, think about what it reminds you of and write down any thoughts that come to mind. Let your intuition guide what you write as you consider how this is connected to your question. Usually, decks have little booklets that have the divinatory explanations of each card, but the great thing about tarot is that you allow it to bring your unconscious to the forefront. So, take your time to think about what the card means to you first, and then, after that, you can take a look at what the booklet says.

Among the questions you can ask before shuffling and pulling a card are: What you need to know for the day, where you are along your journey of healing or a project that matters to you, how you can be of service, what you need to be careful of, and so on.

Three-card Tarot Spreads

These offer you a lot more depth and nuances when it comes to the messages you get from the cards and spirit. Here, you pull three cards instead of one.

Find somewhere quiet and distraction-free. You don't want to be interrupted by anyone. You can decorate this space with crystals, burn incense, or do whatever you need to attract good spiritual energy to the space.

Set your intention. You can bring your question to mind and keep it there, or state it aloud over and over to get yourself in the correct frame of mind. You should choose to address a matter that you have no bias towards so that your personal opinions do not affect what you get. Keep this intention front and center in your mind as you hold the cards in your hands. Don't know what to ask? You can just keep it simple by asking what you need to know.

Shuffle the deck. As you shuffle, continue to state, or think about your intention. Be careful as you shuffle the deck so you don't bend your cards. You can shuffle by cutting your deck into various piles and then stacking them back together in different orders each time. You could spread and scramble all the cards on a flat surface before putting them back together. You can also haphazardly insert a portion of the deck into another haphazardly, over and over.

- **Split the deck into three groups**. They should be as equal to one another as you can get them.
- **Flip the top cards over.** You should be able to see the faces and designs on the cards. Flip them, working from the left stack to the right one.

- **Study the cards.** You can interpret them as the past, the present, and the future, or any other three parameters you want to evaluate regarding what you **need to know.**

- **Feel your cards in your gut.** Take a close look at the designs and see what emotions and thoughts they evoke in you. What impression do you get from them? What colors, shapes, and characters draw you?

- **Interpret your cards.** You can work with the booklet or choose to work using your intuition to discern what it means before referring to the booklet.

Yes/No Spread

This spread is great for yes-or-no questions only. You don't want to ask open-ended questions, and you need to know that this is a great way to make predictions about situations to come or situations that have already happened. You need to think of the predictions not as certainties but as likelihoods.

When a card is upright, that's a yes. When it's drawn reversed, that's a no-no. The way to use this spread is to make sure there's a good balance of reversed and upright cards in your deck. So, you should make sure you cut your deck, flip your cards 180 degrees from top to bottom, and then shuffle them again. Do this several times to have a good balance of reversed and upright cards. If you prefer, you could choose to assign yes and no to various cards in your deck. You can also assign some cards as "maybes" and have them in three piles. Make sure you write down which card represents which answer so that you don't change your mind midway through reading.

1. Have your questions ready, and shuffle your cards as you focus on what you want to know.

2. When you feel ready, fan out the cards on a flat surface, face down.

3. Bring your question to mind again for a moment, and then draw a card. Set this one to your left.

4. Ask the question again (either in your head or out loud), and then draw another card. Put that to the right of the first one.

5. Ask the question one last time, pull out another, and set that to the right.

6. Turn the cards over so you can see if they're a yes, no, or maybe.

7. Reflect on the cards you pulled, especially if you don't get a clear answer.

When you have three yes cards, that's a clear yes. If you have two, you'll get a positive result. If you pick no's and maybe's, your answer is a no. If you find three cards that don't cut it for you, you have the option of pulling five or seven cards for a spread. Don't choose an even number, or you might get muddled answers. However, remember that more isn't better.

Advanced Spreads

The Celtic Cross Spread

This has ten card settings that stand for various questions, and altogether they create a cross with four cards in a vertical row to the right. This is a spread that allows you to really dive into a question more deeply than the other ones we've discussed. It's a classic spread, and it's excellent. It can be rather overwhelming if you're just starting out with the tarot, but the thing is that this is helpful as it will create a context to frame your intuition or question. For instance, drawing the moon tarot card in a position that stands for the querent will lead to a different meaning than when that card takes up a position that has to do with their environment, and so in this way, the Celtic cross spread could be easy to work with and interpret.

- **Begin by shuffling your cards while you focus on your question or intention.** When it comes to the Celtic cross, you should shuffle with your intention in mind or while saying it out loud.

- **Pull 10 cards out and put them in the Celtic cross position.** When you feel you've done enough shuffling, you should split the deck using your left hand, and then you should pick one of the piles and pull 10 of the cards from that pile, starting from the top. Card 1 goes in the middle; card 2 goes on top of it. Cards 3, 4, 5, and 6 go to the top, bottom, left, and right of cards 1 and 2, respectively. Cards 7, 8, 9, and 10 are arranged from the bottom to the top in that order to the right of the cross.

- **Make this spread yours.** When you have the cards out, you can interpret them based on their positions in the spread. We'll talk about what those positions are later on, but you can assign your own meanings to these positions if you want to.

- **Notice any repetition or patterns that show up.** Repeating cards is significant. For instance, if seven shows up a little too often, it could mean you have a lot to contend with to achieve your goal. If you notice too many pentacles, this means you need to think about money and security.

- **Work with your intuition.** You can use your intuition in addition to the traditional interpretations. In fact, you should go with your intuition first and then allow the official descriptions to provide more meaning.

- **Journal your interpretations.** This way, you can refer to them later.

The Positions of the Celtic Cross Spread

Card 1: The Seeker. This is you, and the card you draw in this position applies specifically to you.

Card 2: The Obstacle. This is what is in the way of you getting what you desire.

Card 3: The source. This is the root of the obstacle you're dealing with or the unconscious energy you have that fuels it.

Card 4: The Immediate Past. This is the one that tells you all the things that have transpired lately.

Card 5: Possibilities. This is about available opportunities right now.

Card 6: Your Destination. It's where you're going in the future, and it also shows you the best way to get the results you want.

Card 7: The Way You See Yourself Right Now. Cards seven through ten are read altogether. This card will show you if you think of yourself positively or negatively at the moment.

Card 8: Your Surroundings. It's about where you are, which means the people around you who could be helping or holding you back.

Card 9: Fears and Hopes. This is about your fears and hopes for a circumstance, and not necessarily what will happen, and it's about how you see things.

Card 10: The Result. This is about the outcome, but don't think of it as a hard-set prediction, and it is more to do with where the energy is flowing. The thing about tarot is that, in the end, you have free will, and so you can always change the way you do things to get a different outcome if you don't like what the cards are predicting.

The Horseshoe Spread

The horseshoe is a spread arranged just like a horseshoe or a small letter N. You arrange the cards from 1 to 7, working from the bottom left corner and wrapping up at the bottom right corner. You could also arrange it as a small letter "U," but that's up to you.

- **Set your intention.** Repeat it as you shuffle your cards.
- **Cut your deck.** Keep your intention in mind as you do this. Split it into a pile of three.
- **Pick a pile.** Don't rush this. Take your time and allow your intuition to guide your hand to the right one.
- **Select your cards.** Pick them from the top of the pile of your choosing.
- **Lay them out.** Put each one you pick in the horseshoe arrangement.

Now let's talk about what each card represents.

Card 1: The Past. This is about the influences and events strongly connected to your intention or question, and these influences could be from the recent or distant past.

Card 2: The Present. This is about where you are right now. It's the present situation you're dealing with and the circumstances surrounding it. It's also about the way you think and feels about your question.

Card 3: Hidden Influences. This is about the unseen hands that are guiding the situation. You may not be aware of them, and they could also be the subconscious conflicts and unexpected results that will come. You should also know that this position could represent the future rather than hidden influences.

Card 4: The Obstacles. These are the challenges that are keeping you from resolution. This card could also be used to represent **your attitude** towards the situation or your question.

Card 5: Surroundings. This card is about the environment you're in at the moment, whether physical or mental. It could be a behavior, opinion, or other people's attitudes toward the question in focus.

Card 6: The Best Course of Action. This is about the things you could do to achieve a successful outcome. Sometimes, that could mean doing nothing and allowing things to resolve themselves. Other times, all you need is an attitude adjustment.

Card 7: The Final Result. This is about what is very likely to occur if you follow the guidance of card 6. If you choose to ignore that card, you can also ignore this one.

Extra: Tarot Practice Exercises

Performing Quick Draws

You can use tarot cards just like flashcards. All you have to do for this exercise is flip each card over, one after the other, and then say or write the very first thing that pops into your mind. Don't dawdle, and don't worry about getting this wrong. There are no right or wrong answers here. You can refer to the booklet when you've finished and see if you're close. You can practice this exercise with someone to make it more fun.

Building Spreads

You can put two different decks together, like the tarot and oracle, and then flip the cards on top. Connect the two cards so that they form a story and say or write the very first thing that enters your head. As soon as you feel like you've got the hang of this, you can throw in another deck, or two more, until you're used to reading from several. You can also sort a single deck into its four suits and work on connecting their stories together.

Check-in Using the Cards

This is the process of hitting pause on the daily humdrum to check in with yourself and figure out how you're feeling. The cards are excellent for this, and you can use this method to get more familiar with the minor arcana and numerology.

Give Yourself a Rating

Start by folding a piece of paper so that it has four sides. In each quadrant, write one of the suits of the deck. Under each suit, note down a word that you sense represents the energy of the suit. Next, write down the first thing you've personally experienced that comes into your head when you think of each suit and what it means to you. Keep it to just a sentence or two; the briefer, the better. Next, a rate that experience with a number, with 10 being really good and 1 being really bad. Then check out the meanings of the numbers in this book to see what rating you have for yourself and what it means in each suit. Add the numbers up, reduce them if they're not a master number to a single digit, and see what that means for you as well. Think of the meaning in the context of what each suit stands for. You can also check out the numbers (for each suit and for the total sum) in each minor arcana and notice what the designs of the cards draw from you. Note that the meaning you draw may or may not align with the numerology interpretations, or they may complement one another in curious ways.

Conclusion

In this book, we've offered a comprehensive guide for people interested in starting their own journey of self-discovery and illumination through tarot cards and the history surrounding them. There is a multitude of techniques to help you start figuring out your path, learn how to better it, and find personal fulfillment while going through the process.

Being able to read and decipher the plethora of meanings and signs hidden in the dynamic language of tarot cards can help nudge you in the right direction through your everyday life. Unfortunately, in our current modern context, where we are obsessed with empirically proven facts, tarot reading is being misrepresented and overlooked. However, tarot cards are extremely useful if you're looking for guidance.

If you're confused about a situation or are feeling indecisive about a major step you are about to take, tarot cards can offer a different perspective, illuminate a path of actions or thinking that had previously gone unnoticed by you, or it may even suggest slowing down in certain areas of your everyday life. Every card in a tarot set represents a different aspect of life, and each card lends its own unique take on any situation you need to seek guidance or clarity for. Remember that how you interpret the signs in your card reading depends on your state of mind while in the process, and what you need to focus on or listen to the most.

You definitely don't have to profoundly believe in any higher powers, and it doesn't necessarily have to be a deeply spiritual experience for you to benefit from your reading; but with time and practice, you will find that you are spiritually drawn to the subtle guidance offered by tarot cards; most tarot readers and practitioners appreciate the sheer fact that one's cards usually align with their current life path and seem to offer advice that can be realistically mulled over and tested out. Some practitioners, who read for themselves, understand their interpretations as their subconscious mind or inner intuitive guide at work. It is necessary to read and look through a lot of different sources on the practice and understand its history as you learn how to read tarot cards; this step will help you make more sense of the world you're entering.

Here's another book by Silvia Hill that you might like

Free limited time bonus

Stop for a moment. I have a free bonus set up for you. The problem is that we forget 90% of everything that we read after 7 days. Crazy fact, right? Here's the solution: we've created a printable, 1-page pdf summary for this book that you're reading now. All you have to do to get your free pdf summary is to go to the following website: **https://livetolearn.lpages.co/silviahill/**
Once you do, it will be intuitive. Enjoy, and thank you!

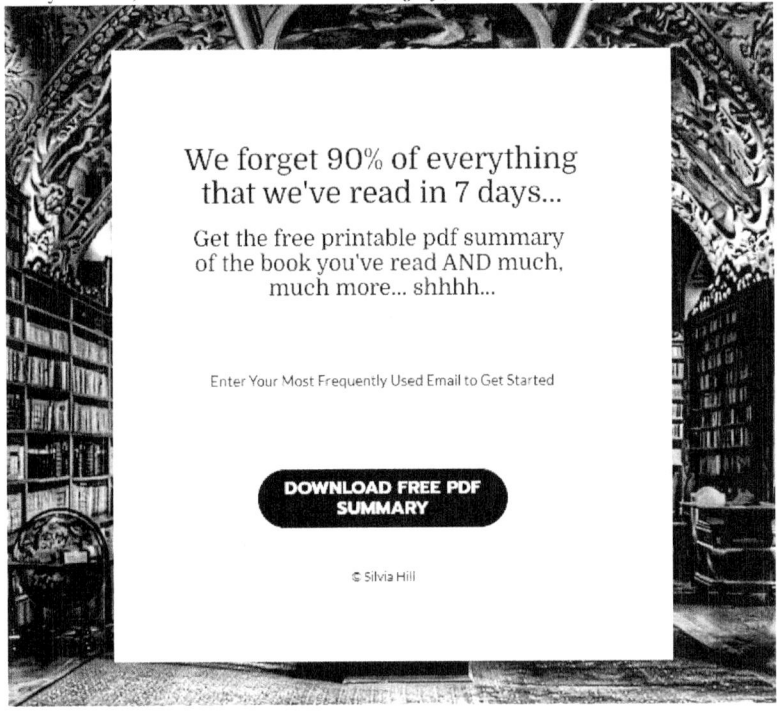

Glossary

Air: An element. Communicative, intellectual, mental, masculine, active.

Air Signs: Aquarius, Libra, Gemini. They are the thinkers.

Aquarius: The water bearer. Connected to the Star card. Led by Uranus. A fixed air sign. Scientific, original, aloof, detached, impersonal unconventional, independent, nonconforming, utopian, visionary, futuristic progressive, humanitarian.

Aries: The ram. In charge of the first house in astrology. Led by Mars. Courageous, commanding, impulsive, assertive, energetic. A cardinal fire sign.

Cancer: The crab. In charge of the 4th house. Led by the moon. Instinctual, intuitive, sympathetic, sentimental, sensitive, protective, nurturing, emotional. A cardinal water sign.

Capricorn: The goat. In charge of the 10th house. Led by Saturn. Ambitious, cautious, persistent, patient, organized, methodical, dutiful, disciplined, responsible, pragmatic. A cardinal earth sign.

Classical Planets: All seven planets are observable with the naked eye. The Sun, Moon, Mercury, Venus, Mars, Jupiter, and Saturn.

Earth: One of the four classical elements.

Earth Signs: Virgo, Taurus, Capricorn.

Fire: One of the four classical elements.

Fire signs: Leo, Sagittarius, Aries.

Horoscope: An English derivative of the Greek words hora and skopos. The astrological chart.

House Ruler: The ruling planet of a house.

Jupiter: Planet of generosity and lack. In charge of Sagittarius and the 9th house. Long journeys, law, religion, higher thoughts, extravagance, prosperity, good fortune.

Leo: The lion. Led by the sun. Ruler of the 5th house. Domineering, creative, proud, dramatic, generous, loyal, warm, regal. A fixed fire sign.

Libra: The scales. A mutable air sign. Indolent, indecisive, harmonious, refined, balanced, fair, cooperative, social, charming, gracious. Ruler of the 7th house, led by Venus.

Mars: Ruler of Aries and the 1st house. The initiative, will, drive, passion, desire, courage, aggression, assertiveness, action, energy.

Mercury: Planet of communication and speed. Ruler of the 3rd and 6th houses, and Virgo and Gemini. Speech, writing, wit, reason, logic.

Moon Phases: New moon, waxing moon, full moon, waning moon.

Moon: In charge of the 4th house and cancer. Motherhood, mood, memory, emotion, life cycles, inner life reflection.

Mutable Signs: Virgo, Pisces, Gemini, Sagittarius. These signs are flexible.

Natal Chart: Horoscope plotted by observing the planets' positions relative to each other at the birth location, time, and date.

Neptune: Leads the 12th house and Pisces. Deception, confusion, sacrifice, escapism, idealism, spirituality, illusion, dreams, imagination.

New Moon: Dark moon that starts a lunar month.

Pisces: The fish. A mutable water sign. Leads the 12th house. Led by Neptune. Victimized or victimizing, secretive, illusionary, empathetic, impressionable, self-sacrificing, compassionate, imaginative.

Pluto: In charge of Scorpio and the 8th house. Analysis, compulsion, power, elimination, destruction, death, endings, unavoidable change, regeneration, transformation.

Sagittarius: The Archer. A mutable fire sign led by Jupiter. In charge of the 9th house. Tactlessness, candidness, enthusiasm, optimism, philosophy, adventure.

Saturn: In charge of the 10th house and Capricorn. Old age, authority, father figures, delay, inhibition, ambition, control, caution, discipline, structure, restriction, responsibility, limitations, boundaries.

Scorpio: The Scorpion. A fixed water sign. Led by Pluto. In charge of the 8th house. Life's dark mysteries are psychic, intimate, possessive, strong will, passionate, introspective, jealous, secretive, penetrating, intense.

Sun: In charge of the 5th house and Leo. Fatherhood, authority, pride, individuality, vitality, purpose, will, ego, self.

Taurus: The Bull. A fixed earth sign. In charge of the 2nd house. Led by Venus. Practical, stable, patient, sensual, security conscious, possessive, materialistic, stubborn, determined.

Uranus: In charge of the 11th house and Aquarius. Futurism, originality, technology, revolution, disruption, sudden change.

Venus: In charge of the 2nd house, as well as the 7th house. Values, harmony, artistry, affection, beauty, love.

Virgo: The Virgin. A mutable earth sign. Ruled by Mercury. In charge of the 6th house. Critical, health-conscious, productive, discriminating, organized, detail-oriented, practical, analytical.

Waning Moon: The moon as it goes from full to dark or new.

Water: One of the four classical elements.

Water Signs: Cancer, Pisces, Scorpio.

Waxing Moon: The moon as it goes from new to full.

Zodiac: The space belt surrounding earth, split into twelve signs; the heavenly bodies that move from west to east, moving through sign after sign starting from Aries and ending at Pisces.

References

Bunning, Joan. Learning the Tarot (Boston: Red Wheel/Weiser, 1998).

Burk, Kevin. Understanding the Birth Chart (Woodbury, MN: Llewellyn Worldwide, 2001).

Decker, Ronald, and Michael Dummet. A History of the Occult Tarot: 1870-1970 (London:

Gerald Duckworth & Co. Ltd., 2002).

DuQuette, Lon Milo. Understanding Aleister Crowley's Thoth Tarot (San Francisco: Red

Wheel/Weiser, 2003).

Frawley, John. The Real Astrology (London: Apprentice Books, 2001).

Gerwick-Brodeur, Madeline and Lisa Lenard. The Complete Idiot's Guide to Astrology (New

York: Alpha Books, 1997).

Gurney, Joseph. "The Tarot of the Golden Dawn." Journal of the Western Mystery Tradition (No. 17, Vol. 2, Autumnal Equinox 2009).

Guttman, Ariel, and Kenneth Johnson. Mythic Astrology: Archetypal Powers in the Horoscope (Woodbury, MN: Llewellyn Worldwide, 1996).

Hampar, Joann. Astrology for Beginners: A Simple Way to Read Your Chart (Woodbury, MN: Llewellyn Worldwide, 2007).

Hulse, David Allen. The Key to It All, Book Two: The Western Mysteries (Woodbury, MN: Llewellyn Worldwide, 1996).

Huson, Paul. Mystical Origins of the Tarot (Rochester, VT: Destiny Books, 2004).

Kenner, Corrine. Simple Fortunetelling with Tarot Cards. (Woodbury, MN: Llewellyn Worldwide, 2007).

Louis, Anthony. Tarot Plain and Simple (Woodbury, MN: Llewellyn Worldwide, 2002).

MacGregor, Trish. The Everything Astrology Book (Holbrook, Massachusetts: Adams Media Corporation, 1999).

Masino, Marcia. Easy Tarot Guide (San Diego: ACS Publications, 1987).

Michelson, Teresa C. The Complete Tarot Reader: Everything You Need to Know from Start to Finish (Woodbury, MN: Llewellyn Worldwide, 2005).

Moore, Barbara. Tarot for Beginners (Woodbury, MN: Llewellyn Worldwide, 2010).

Pollack, Rachel. Tarot Wisdom (Woodbury, MN: Llewellyn Worldwide, 2009)

Printed in Great Britain
by Amazon

79548641R00142